BUILDING

WITH

SECONDHAND

STUFF

BUILDING WITH SECONDHAND STUFF

HOW TO RE-CLAIM, RE-VAMP, RE-PURPOSE & RE-USE SALVAGED & LEFTOVER BUILDING MATERIALS

CHRIS PETERSON

Creative Publishing
international

Creative Publishing international

Copyright © 2011
Creative Publishing international, an imprint of Quarto Publishing Group USA Inc., 400 First Avenue North, Suite 400, Minneapolis, Minnesota 55401
www.creativepub.com
All rights reserved

Printed in China

16 15 14 13 12

Library of Congress Cataloging-in-Publication Data on file

ISBN:978-1-58923-662-2

President/CEO: Ken Fund
Group Publisher: Bryan Trandem

Home Improvement Group

Associate Publisher: Mark Johanson
Managing Editor: Tracy Stanley
Creative Director: Michele Lanci
Art Direction/Design: Brad Springer,
    Kim Winscher, James Kegley
Lead Photographer: Corean Komarec
Shop Manager: James Parmeter
Production Managers: Laura Hokkanen, Linda Halls

Author: Chris Peterson
Page Layout Artist: Kathy Littfin
Shop Help: Charles Boldt
Illustrator: Melanie Powell
Proofreader: Drew Siqveland
Cover photo: istockphoto.com

PHOTO CREDITS

Alamy: 12 bottom (RJH_RF); 13 bottom (Elizabeth Whiting & Associates); 15 top (Marnie Burkhart/Fancy); 90 (Chris Howes/Wild Places Photography); 134 top (Susan Isakson); 138 (cello).

American Tin Ceiling Company: 75.

Dreamstime.com: 14 top, 23 top, 36 top, 78, 95 middle, 109 bottom, 120 top, 124 middle.

iStockphoto.com: 6 center, 8, 18, 25, 30 bottom, 31 middle, 63 top, 93 middle, 111 top, 119 middle, 123 bottom, 124 bottom, 135 bottom, 136 top, 137.

Photolibrary: 6 top middle (Imagesource); 21 bottom (Warwick Kent); 26 (Erick Saillet/Photononstop); 62 middle (Photoshot); 116 (Glow Décor).

Shutterstock.com: 12 top, 16, 17 bottom, 22 right, 23 bottom, 24, 30 top & second from bottom, 32 top & bottom, 33 bottom, 34 top, 36 bottom, 37 top & bottom, 45, 46 bottom, 60 right, 62 top & bottom, 68 bottom, 72, 74, 76, 84, 92, 93 top & bottom, 94 top, 95 top & bottom, 103 right bottom, 104, 109 top, 110, 111 bottom, 114, 117 top, 118 top, 119 bottom, 120 bottom, 121, 122, 123 top, 124 top, 132, 139.

CONTENTS

Introduction

—⁓—

Millions of new structures are built across America every single year. Homes fill brand new housing developments, office buildings go up to serve corporate expansion, and even a few new barns are constructed. Meanwhile, hundreds of thousands of old buildings are razed. Other older structures are simply abandoned and left to the ravages of time. The cast-offs, the buildings being replaced or simply removed, are usually quickly demolished and sent to the nearest dump. But that truly is a waste. These buildings represent a fantastic opportunity to help the environment, save a little money, and incorporate one-of-kind design elements into your home.

Many—if not most—of the components that went into building structures that are ready to come down can be salvaged to find new life as reused home-design and building components. Using reclaimed building materials in new ways is part of a larger movement of sustainable building practices. In contrast to demolition, which sends tons of debris to landfills, this environmentally friendly process is called "deconstruction." Deconstruction is the craft of taking apart the structure to preserve every piece that can be reused, repurposed, or recycled. It's one aspect of environmentally friendly living. But the rewards of reclaiming building materials and reusing them in your home extend far beyond helping the environment. That just happens to be arguably the most important benefit.

AN EASY GREEN SOLUTION

Landfills are filling up quicker than we can find new places to put our building debris and other garbage. We produce more waste per person than any other country on the planet. We're also consuming materials at an alarming rate. Old growth forests have been overlogged for centuries, and now precious few are left. The U.S. Environmental Protection Agency estimates that we simply throw away more than a billion board feet of lumber each year. If we reused all of that we could save more than a million trees each year. Large deposits of high-quality quarry stones such as granite and marble are harder and harder to find. There's simply no getting around that fact that many of the materials we've come to associate with quality in the home are either non-renewable or very slow to renew. And those resources continue to be depleted.

Diminishing natural resources are not the only environmental repercussions of our ongoing hunt for building materials. Finding, harvesting, and getting those materials to market means using vast amounts of energy. That translates to massive quantities of fossil fuels consumed—and pollution created—in the process. It's a cold, hard fact that the buildings we erect tend to cost much more than we pay for them.

Fortunately, there are many solutions to the environmental issues raised in producing new building materials. Increasingly, builders and contractors are using synthetic and recycled alternatives, or extremely renewable resources such as bamboo. Home building and design are becoming more efficient, and other solutions will no doubt arise in the future. But a big answer to the issue of environmental impact and limited resources comes from the past. There is a treasure trove of usable materials in the buildings we tear down (or that fall down of their own accord). We just need to tap that resource.

Building debris accounts for much of the waste clogging landfills—most of which could actually be put back into use.

These Douglas fir timbers were rescued from a building about to be demolished. Now they'll be repurposed as mantels, counters, or even support beams, providing unique beauty and a tremendous bargain for lucky homeowners.

LOWER COST, HIGHER QUALITY

Saving the environment could easily be a good enough justification to salvage and reuse building materials. But there are other great reasons as well—saving a little money chief among them. The mini-industry that has sprung up to reclaim and resell used building materials competes with home centers and other retailers based largely on lower price and higher quality. Depending on whether you're shopping for heritage wood flooring or looking for a rescued slate slab for a countertop, you can expect to save from 10 to 50 percent off the price of comparable material sold brand new. In some instances, the owner of a building that must come down will let you take whatever you can safely remove, so the materials you salvage will cost nothing more than your labor.

Regardless of the source, you can expect to walk away with material that is as good or better quality than what you would pick up in the aisles of your local home center. Just about the only downside is that it may entail more research and work on your part, and much of what you find will not be in the standardized measurements common to building materials today.

Still, your wallet will thank you. And the money you save will be just part of your reward. Certain qualities and types of materials—especially woods—are no longer available. Rare types of quarry stone, finely detailed architectural accents, and handcrafted leaded windows are just a sampling of the treasures that can't

be matched on today's marketplace. In fact, much of the increasing popularity of reclaimed building materials is due to their unique nature and singular beauty. If you're in search of a one-of-a-kind look, reclaimed materials are a great place to start.

You may find rare species of woods not available, unusual stone surfaces with patterns and colors you're not likely to come across anywhere else, and glass that bears elegant imperfections from a less-standardized manufacturing process. Or maybe you're looking for something more modest, such as faucet or door handles that capture the charm of an earlier time, or wrought iron grillwork that can be repurposed as an eye-catching fence or bench.

Whatever the reclaimed material, small design projects are a great place to start reusing them. Although building an entire home or large structure from reclaimed materials takes a great deal of dedication and planning, and requires specialized expertise, the projects we've collected for this book can be completed by any homeowner with modest DIY skills and a basic set of tools. We've purposely selected projects that are versatile and adaptable to any home. The techniques described here will provide a good base of skills and knowledge for working with any reclaimed materials, no matter what state they're in or what you want to do with them. Start with these projects and eventually you'll find even more ways to salvage and save.

GALLERY OF SALVAGED BUILDING MATERIALS

A mantelpiece made of reclaimed hand-hewn oak timbers is the perfect complement to a fireplace surround of reclaimed stacked fieldstone and a hearth of salvaged slate. The combination of elements is visually impressive and likely to last the life of the home and beyond.

Antique, high-grade reclaimed heart pine flooring is the perfect surface for a kitchen featuring cabinetry with a distressed finish. The floor was finished clear to allow the wonderful properties of the grain to shine through.

Salvaged terra cotta floor tiles provide a newly remodeled kitchen with a visually warm, charming, and incredibly durable floor.

Granite "curbstone" blocks wait for the right opportunity to show off their beautiful and indestructible nature—perhaps as a fireplace base.

Reclaimed materials don't necessarily have to be reclaimed from defunct buildings. This gorgeous redwood table was crafted from a slab cut from a huge fallen tree. The tree was salvaged, having fallen naturally.

A restored stained glass window sparkles like new in an opening that once housed a plain double-hung unit. It's an entirely unique decorative element.

An antique doorknob is the only hardware that really looks right on an antique door. In most cases they can be used with modern door latch mechanisms.

A rich floor of mixed species barnwood provides an incredible stage for modern decor. Notice that the homeowner has used exposed rough-sawn beams in the space as well, adding to textural complexity and visual excitement.

Antique lighting fixtures are often unlike anything on the marketplace. Inside or out, they make for stunning— and functional— focal points.

A mix of reclaimed teak and barnwood was used to build this rustic cabinet. The barn-wood was left unfinished and the surface is a mix of textures and colors that invites the hands as well as the eyes.

Even hardware can be reclaimed for distinctive accents on kitchen cabinetry, doors, and windows.

Reclaimed fieldstone and firebox bricks make for a memorable and fitting fireplace surround. Antique timbers create the perfect mantel for this structure.

The amazing grain pattern of a reclaimed curly redwood slab turns this simple table into a showpiece. Crafting the table was largely just a matter of cleaning and refinishing the wood, and adding handcrafted, bentwood legs.

Vintage windows can be a lovely element in a room addition. Re-glaze the windows correctly and the insulation value will approach that of new single-pane units.

Chapter I

—⚋—

WORKING WITH RECLAIMED MATERIALS

Open up to the potential of salvaged building products and you give yourself an incredible variety of design possibilities. You can create a showcase fireplace with a granite curbstone mantel. Fashion a unique kitchen backsplash from a recovered and refinished tin ceiling. Add a distinctive element to your living room with a hickory plank floor, or lay an enchanted pathway through your garden as a way to recycle a pallet of turn-of-the century cobblestones. Even more uses lie waiting in the closet of your imagination. Once you discover all the options available, you'll probably wonder why anyone would ever choose to use new building materials.

Incredible diversity—not only among available materials, but between similar pieces as well—is at the heart of what makes salvaged materials so attractive. Time leaves its mark on all of us, but no more so than on the stone, wood, metal, and glass we build with. These materials age gracefully, featuring patinas of intriguing colors and patterns unlike anything you would find on newer products. Older building materials are often irregular, with imperfections that actually add to their appearances. You'll be amazed at the different looks even among the same types of wood, or two similar bricks or stones.

Your search for the ideal building material that will bring your design project to life begins with the actual material you're considering. Whether it's a stunning antique door to replace a bland entryway, a new countertop, or a bedroom floor, you'll need to narrow down the myriad options. There are actually three different types of goods commonly salvaged from buildings: Small architectural accents such as hooks, corbels, doorknobs, and hinges; single-piece fixtures including cabinet units, doors, and windows; and raw materials such as timbers, flooring and stones.

CHOOSING AMONG SALVAGED MATERIALS

The actual reclaimed material you'll be looking for will of course be determined by your project. Some, such as a new fireplace mantel, can be crafted of different materials, from barn timbers to granite curbstones. Others, such as a living room floor, lend themselves to only one type of material. And you shouldn't discount newer salvaged pieces. Some reclaimed building materials come from more recent buildings that are being extensively renovated and can present opportunities for intact building elements that are cheaper and just as good as new.

DECONSTRUCTION TOOLS

Square blade shovel (A); Sledge hammer (B); Hand maul (C); Pry bars (D); Claw hammer (E); "Cat's paw" nail puller (F); Utility knife (G); End-cut pliers (H); Extractor pliers (I); Locking-jaw pliers (J); Metal detector (K); Circuit tester (L); Combination stud sensor/laser level (M); Voltmeter (N); Cordless drill bit assortments (O); Pick axe (P); Circular saw (Q); Reciprocating saw (R)

WOOD

This is the most commonly salvaged material because it is so ubiquitous in both old and new construction. You can reuse wood from all the different areas of a building, including siding, structural timbers, existing wood flooring, and interior paneling. The wood can be used as is, with the scars and marks of use in full display, or it can be resized and refinished to look brand new. Wood pieces can even be milled to serve new purposes, such as reconstituting solid-wood paneling boards into tongue-and-groove flooring. Old wood can find new life as tables, shelves, countertops, mantels, flooring, siding, and more. Entire wood structures, such as doors and shutters, are commonly resized and fitted for service in existing openings.

MASONRY

Many different types of stone and bricks are used inside and outside of buildings. Other types are used to pave roads and paths, and provide edging for sidewalks. All of these can be repurposed to stunning effect, in a number of different areas of your home. Fireplace surrounds and mantels are extremely common uses for reclaimed stone. Depending on the architectural and decorative style of your house, cobblestones or certain pavers can make a lovely kitchen floor. Exclusive quarry stones like granite, marble, and travertine can be used as stunning countertops or custom tabletops. Salvaged pavers and bricks are perhaps most at home outside, where they can be used to create a charming pathway through the garden or yard.

METAL

Metals such as iron and copper are regularly rescued from buildings being demolished. But because they are generally inexpensive and are so easily recycled, most salvaged metals find their way into the smelter. However, certain types of metal fixtures are well-suited to be repurposed as new home-design elements. Plumbing pipes and sheet forms such as tin ceilings are prime examples of metal pieces that can easily be adapted into a room design. You can cover an accent wall with hammered sheet metal or copper tiles for an arresting decorative feature. Use a heating vent grill to craft a coffee table, or make shelves or a pot hanger from copper pipes.

GLASS & CERAMICS

Most salvaged glass is reused for home design in the form of windows. The unusual shapes of some antique windows, and the classic look of leaded glass windows, make those options particularly popular. But you don't have to limit yourself. Stained glass designs are also regularly rescued, rehabilitated and reinstalled in new locations.

SOURCING RECLAIMED MATERIALS

Once you've made the decision to use salvaged wood, stone, or other reclaimed building material in a home-design project, the next step is to track down a good source. The bad news is that finding the perfect timbers for a trestle table, the right slab of marble to use for a new countertop, or a modestly sized leaded glass window to put in that interior partition wall won't be quite as simple as heading out to the local home center. The good news is that you do have a lot of different resources to turn to in your search. And many of those represent the opportunity to negotiate an enviable price for your treasure.

Frankly, there are a lot of different sources for reclaimed building materials. Each has its benefits and drawbacks. The one you use will depend first and foremost on the type of material you're after. You'll also need to decide just how much work you're willing to do. Getting your hands on some materials can entail getting those hands a little dirty. You may be faced with the prospect of picking up the material if it's not local, or arranging for shipment. You may have to clean, revive, and prep the material before use. No matter what the case, always consider the full range of potential suppliers before making a decision.

RETAIL AND WHOLESALE SALVAGE COMPANIES

The past two decades have seen a steady growth in the number of companies reselling materials salvaged from demolished or renovated buildings. At the high-end are companies that deal primarily in architectural antiques, artifacts and intact period structures such as decorative plaster corbels or hand-carved marble fireplace surrounds. The broader middle part of the market is populated by general salvage firms dealing in raw building materials such as barn timbers and large curbstones. Some of these companies clean and prepare their inventory, while others simply reclaim and stock the materials, selling them as is. Most usually specialize in a specific substance such as wood or stone, although many stock whatever materials come their way, and their inventories fluctuate accordingly. This is why looking for the material that's ideal for your project can be a little like a scavenger hunt. These companies should be your first stop. They're generally professional and easy to deal with. They can set up shipping if the need arises, and in most cases, you can rely on the integrity of the materials.

DEFUNCT STRUCTURES

If you have access to a dilapidated building, along with good DIY skills, knowledge of how buildings go together, and a solid selection of tools, you may choose to deconstruct and reclaim all or part of the building yourself. This can be a remarkably inexpensive way to recover building materials of all sorts—including hidden gems. You may, for example, find wood flooring in a beautiful antique species hidden under ratty old carpet. But local codes and regulations dictate safety practices (you should exercise appropriate safety measures in any case) and disposal methods that must be used in demolition or deconstruction. Some situations, such as the removal of asbestos, require extremely involved abatement procedures. Encountering toxic materials is one of the downsides to deconstruction, and abating material such as asbestos insulation can quickly escalate your costs.

CONTRACTORS AND DEMOLITION COMPANIES

Buildings don't necessarily have to be taken entirely apart for them to produce materials worthy of recycling. Simple jobs such as a bathroom renovation can create piles of usable tiles, flooring, and pipes. A bigger home renovation can result in healthy quantities of antique wood flooring, cast-iron heating vent grills, or other desirables. Generally, however, it's not worth a contractor's time to carefully remove and resuscitate old tile or flooring. It's much easier to simply rip out the material and send it on a trip to the dump, never to be seen again. If you're willing to do a significant amount of work, you may be able to make a deal with a contractor: you provide the labor to demo the space, and in return, you keep the materials you remove. This is not an arrangement that suits everyone, but it can be a great way to lay your hands on unique building materials in exchange for sweat equity. In other cases, you may be able to work with large demolition companies to strip a building of valuable commodities before the company tears it down (or even as part of tearing it down). This type of arrangement works best when you need a large amount of wood, metal, or stone. It's not, however, for the uninitiated. Just as with deconstructing a building yourself, working in a job site space requires adhering to local regulations and codes and the same safety issues apply. You can make your life easier by limiting your agreement to combing through the roll-on dumpsters at the job site. The best way to get in on the process from the beginning is when safety fences go up around a job site, or you see work permits appear in the windows of an older house.

ONLINE RESOURCES

The Internet has made selling small quantities of reclaimed building materials easy and simple. Even individuals can offer leftovers from renovations or building deconstructions, on websites such as Craigslist or Ebay. Of course, buying from someone who isn't operating as a business and doesn't have a professional reputation to protect entails a certain amount of risk—especially if that source isn't local. You have to be cautious that you're actually getting the quality and specifications that the seller advertised. In-person inspection is always the best way to go. On the upside, materials sold online often offer incredible deals. Sometimes they are even offered free to anyone willing to haul them away.

GARAGE SALES, SWAP MEETS AND FLEA MARKETS

This is the most hit-or-miss resource. But if you're willing to put in a fair amount of legwork, you can often stumble upon hidden treasures. Be prepared to haul away whatever you find, and come equipped with a measuring tape to determine if the dimensions of whatever it is suit the project you have in mind. The informal nature of these types of venues lends itself to healthy negotiation and great deals. You can find notices of garage and yard sales in local newspapers—also a great place to look for individuals selling material through the classifieds.

ASSESSING WHAT YOU FIND

Once you've found a reliable source, the next step is to judge if the material itself is worth repurposing. Know the history of the donor building. This is especially important if you're looking at reclaimed wood or unsealed stone. It's just a basic health and safety issue. For instance, unfinished stone or wood used in an early-twentieth-century factory may have been exposed to high levels of toxic chemicals. Much as you may love the look and price of the material, any stone or wood that was exposed to toxic or carcinogenic chemicals needs to be properly disposed of, not reused in a home.

Suffice it to say, it's well worth your while to ask questions and investigate as necessary to determine the history of whatever you're considering for reuse. Once you're certain the stone, wood, or metal isn't going to be a health problem, check the actual quality of the material. Judge the structural integrity, and look for obvious signs of damage, such as cracking, checking, or wear that would make reuse problematic. Check wood flooring for screw and nail holes too numerous to cover up with a little putty. Be diligent in looking for insect

Although you shouldn't judge reclaimed material on first impressions, you do need to use a critical eye when shopping for these materials. Some will have been subject to the elements so long that their integrity is compromised. Others will have been exposed to toxic substances. Wood such as this reclaimed from a water tank needs to be checked for both.

damage, even if it doesn't mar the appearance. For instance, wood timbers that look fine on the surface but have been structurally weakened throughout by termite damage are perhaps not a wise choice for a table or other load-bearing application. Unless you're willing to cut them down for reuse, cracked window glass and broken terra cotta tiles should also be recycled, not repurposed.

In addition to basic structural integrity, look at the amount of preparation that will be required to make the material project-ready. For instance, old weathered redwood siding may look beaten up and too far gone to restore it to its original beauty, but a simple powerwashing can revive the appearance. Aged bricks can be beautiful, colored with a timeworn patina that makes the surface of each one unique and fascinating. But if the bricks you've chosen are checkered with stubborn cement-based mortar, you may have considerable difficulty removing the mortar without destroying the brick.

SALVAGE WISDOM: RECLAIMING ARCHITECTURAL ACCENTS

No discussion of designing with reclaimed materials is complete without a mention of rescued architectural bits and pieces. These range from glass doorknobs that can add a lovely and elegant touch to doors throughout a home, to hinges and handles that can dress up plain wood cabinets, to the much rarer, more special, and more expensive ornamentation such as plaster pediments and wooden finials. There are many companies that offer reclaimed architectural ornaments from both the U.S. and Europe, although detailed fixtures such as decorative corbels can be quite pricey. However, in most cases, using small accents is one sure way to add big flair to your house without a big price tag.

Chapter 2

—⁓—

RECLAIMING HERITAGE WOOD

Wood, in all its many forms, is the most commonly salvaged building material. That should come as no surprise because it's one of the most attractive materials used in a home. It makes for an unrivaled surface underfoot, a warm and visually pleasant wall covering, a dramatic countertop choice, and so much more. Wood is also incredibly durable and forgiving, sturdy, and easy to work with. All of which is why most buildings feature wood framing. Some structures, such a barns and other utility buildings, are constructed solely of this compelling material. Start taking apart a building, or even a part of a building, and you'll be rewarded with a variety of wood pieces that you can reuse in a vast number of ways. Once you free it from its current location, you have only to decide what new use will best exploit the particular size, grain, texture, and color of the wood.

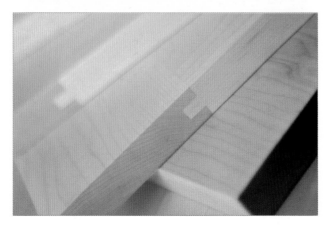

CHERRY

Cherry wood constitutes a very small proportion of the new hardwood produced (most of it used in furniture building), making old buildings a primary source for this distinctive wood. The wood has long been—and continues to be—favored by cabinetmakers and other furniture builders for its subtle beauty. The heartwood features a rich red to reddish-brown that deepens as the wood ages. The grain is elegantly uniform and fine, broken up occasionally by small imperfections. Although the wood is most commonly used in furniture, it is also a superior and very desirable plank flooring.

ANTIQUE ELM

Featuring a more subtle look than other hardwoods, heartwood elm features sophisticated colors ranging from tan to a red-tinted brown, and an understated flowing grain pattern that doesn't call attention to itself. The elm population in this country has been largely devastated by Dutch Elm disease, so this is another hardwood usually only found as reclaimed material. It has seen wide use in furniture making, millwork and paneling (and is a traditional wood for wood caskets). It's also an excellent flooring option, especially where a slightly more understated surface is preferred. Many people use reclaimed pieces for paneling.

HICKORY

This is yet another very rare and beautiful hardwood. Hickory—the fruit-bearing species is the pecan tree—is one of the hardest, toughest, and longest-wearing woods you can find. These properties are why it's the traditional wood of choice for tool handles, and what makes the wood an ideal flooring. Colors run from the pale, nearly white sapwood, to the dark, red-brown of the heartwood. The grain is tight and straight except for rare exceptions, when it can be enticingly wavy. The wood's texture is coarse. You can expect a hickory plank floor to last the life of the building, if not the lifetime of the occupants.

MAPLE

You'll find maple on the floors, walls, and in the furniture of once-opulent houses dating as far back as two centuries. The source of famously sweet maple syrup, the wood has long been favored for its deep creamy white color, accented by fine flowing grain. Some species sport curly grains, while the namesake Bird's-eye Maple offers an endlessly intriguing circular grain. The wood is very hard, dense, and strong, and has seen use as Native American spears, the heels for women's shoes, and as high-quality cutting boards.

You can reclaim pieces for use as paneling, flooring, or high-exposure applications such as the skirting around a kitchen island—or even to make shelves or other furnishings. However, the hard surface resists wear so well that it's even been used as a bowling alley surface—which is why reclaimed maple is most often used as flooring.

ANTIQUE OAK

You can reclaim this lovely wood from old flooring and interior paneling. The grain is pronounced and aged varieties tend to have a deep honey tone that can run from gold to rich milk-chocolate brown, with irregular dark swirls that are sometimes referred to as "tiger stripes." Much of the old oak you find will include knots and other imperfections that are considered part of its beauty. Vintage oak is most often reused as flooring, in either plank or strip forms. Planks can be ripped to width as desired, or as damage to the wood dictates. Tongue or grooves can be re-milled in the ripped side. Oak reclaimed directly from the source is usually refinished with a clear sealer such as polyurethane, to allow the grain, surface variations, and age patina to show through.

WALNUT

This traditional furniture wood is also a captivating species in flooring, paneling, and for cabinet cases and doors. The heartwood is a sumptuous, deep, almost-chocolate brown, while sapwood is the color of brown sugar. The colors of the wood mellow intriguingly with age, and the grain patterns vary from fairly straight to incredibly wavy. The most sought-after type is black walnut, but all walnut is rare in buildings and is most often reclaimed from dilapidated barns that were built with wood from trees on the property.

WHITE OAK

As with most hardwood species, white oak sapwood is lighter than the heartwood, but not by much. Even the heartwood is light to tan, and the graining is very tight—especially in the older wood that is most often reclaimed. The color of older white oak can deepen to a beautiful, rich golden tone. Otherwise, the appearance of the wood is elegant if undistinguished. Although more commonly used than some other hardwoods, white oak was historically dedicated to cask and barrel construction. You are most likely to come across white oak in older homes, in the form of cabinets that (if not structurally damaged) can be refinished to a glowing splendor, casework and moldings, and paneling that can be used as is, or repurposed into flooring.

SALVAGE WISDOM: TOBACCO BARN WOOD

Wood used in dated tobacco-curing barns is some of the most unique you'll ever work with. Traditional curing barns were built from the 18th through the mid-20th centuries. More modern structures were put into widespread use in the 1970s, making most of the older curing barns obsolete. The wood planks used to build older barns were of mixed species, usually a result of having several different types of trees nearby. The species in any given barn may include antique pine, hemlock, cypress, and others. The tobacco-curing process used in these barns involved maintaining charcoal fires at temperatures in excess of 100°F. Over time, the heated smoke impregnated the barn boards, often more than ½ inch below the surface. This resulted in a range of intense, captivating colors that were different board to board and barn to barn. Resellers deconstruct the barns and surface the boards just enough to create a smooth and level face, often milling them with tongues and grooves.

You can do the same if you have access to an old tobacco-curing barn, although the structures are now rare and resellers are often your best bet for large amounts of the wood. Tobacco-barn wood is not only beautiful, but the colorations are entirely unique, creating a one-of-kind appearance for paneling, doors, stairs, molding or flooring.

TYPES OF RECLAIMED LUMBER

TIMBERS AND BEAMS

The most plentiful reclaimed lumber comes in the form of various-sized structural members. The most impressive are the large timbers rescued from barns, warehouses, and other old rustic structures. These are often visually fascinating, scarred with the original marks of the instrument used to square them off. The timbers can run 2 foot square or larger, and are sometimes 20 feet long. Smaller beams can be just as impressive, and headers 4 to 6 inches thick are common as well. The beauty of large timbers is that they can fill both practical and aesthetic roles. They can be used in their original form for a rough, rustic look, or resurfaced and refinished to serve as a sleek exposed structural element in a home. Smaller members are often used for making tables or other furnishings, including built-ins such as bookshelves. Framing members of intriguing wood species can be laminated, sawn, and finished to craft remarkable countertops.

PLANKS

Wood planks are reclaimed from the floors of large structures such as warehouses, and the siding of old homes, barns, and rural outbuildings. The planks can be used in a number of ways. Depending on where the planks come from, how they were originally cut, and what surface appearance aging has left on them, the planks can be used as is, lightly surfaced and refinished to retain the marks of age, or completely resurfaced to recapture the original grain pattern and color. Planks are most often squared off or milled shiplap. But plain planks can be milled to serve as tongue-and-groove flooring or paneling. They can also be ripped to produce strip flooring.

FLOORING

Much of the usable wood recovered from older buildings is flooring. Because plank flooring was the more common style prior to the mid-20th century, most reclaimed wood flooring comes in the form of planks. The planks can be tongue-and-groove, shiplapped, or butt joined. Shiplapped is more common the older the building is, because it was easier to manufacture. Older wide planks are also usually longer than today's strips, often running 8 feet or longer. Squared planks such as siding are generally milled with a tongue-and-groove before being used for a new floor. Think twice before ripping planks to create strip floors; the wider surface of a plank allows for more of the grain and coloring to show.

DOORS

Reclaimed doors can add wonderful flair to different areas of a home, from the kitchen to the front entryway. Doors salvaged from older buildings are usually solid wood in the same interesting grains and colors you'll find on planks, timbers, and flooring. Door styles are nearly limitless, with arched single and double doors a common find. Doors to fit more standard openings are available in just about every panel configuration imaginable. You'll find older interior doors as well, including solid pocket doors, and doors with leaded glass inserts. Other varieties include handcrafted closet doors, and some contemporary solid wood doors (hollow-core doors are rarely reclaimed). Shutters in all shapes and sizes are an intriguing offshoot of this category and can be adapted for use as cabinet doors or decoration. The trick to reusing any found door is choosing one that is the right shape and close to the measurements of the opening you're looking to fill. Then it's just a case of trimming and refitting the door for its new role. This is can be a major job when retrofitting a front door, and less so when replacing kitchen cabinet doors.

RECLAIMED WOOD TEXTURES

Surface texture is another of the many unique qualities that separate reclaimed wood from new lumber. Some older lumber will have a perfectly smooth surface. But you'll also find many other textures on the wood you salvage or find at a reseller. Older machinery and wood-processing techniques often left the wood's surface marked in unusual ways. The time, effort, and expense necessary to completely finish the surface was usually prohibitive or considered unnecessary. These days, those manufacturing marks are valued as evidence of history and character.

ROUGH SAWN

Rough sawing is the first stage of several in milling a piece of lumber. Wood mills have historically left certain support timbers and other structural members rough sawn to save time and money. This was especially true in the lumber used to construct barns, warehouses, and other purely functional buildings, where precise measurements and polished appearances didn't matter. Both hardwoods and softwoods were left rough sawn. Today, the coarse look and rough texture of a rough-sawn piece of lumber can lend a novel decorative element to a home, as long as it's used thoughtfully. Rough-sawn planks are wonderful rustic paneling in a den, and rough-sawn timbers provide a remarkable focal point when incorporated as exposed support beams, posts, or headers. In any case, the texture is best used sparingly in home design and it should be left unfinished and unpainted.

CIRCLE SAWN

Circle saws were used in mills before the advent of modern mill machinery. The process leaves regularly spaced, clearly apparent arcs across the face of cut boards. Circle saw marks are considered handsome proof of age, and make for an extraordinary look in paneling, tables, and flooring. Circle-sawn lumber can be lightly sanded for refinishing without diminishing the impact of the saw marks.

SKIP SAWN

A predecessor to circle sawing, skip sawing creates much the same marks as you would find on a circle-sawn board, except that the marks are more random. It is a more informal and rustic look, but used in the right situation, it can be a very attractive surface texture for floors or wall paneling.

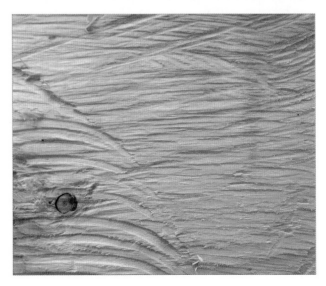

HAND HEWN

This term refers to timbers cut by hand with an adze or axe, and worked with other tools to create support beams and timbers. Found only in very old structures, hand-hewn timbers are usually hardwoods or softwoods from trees felled on the site, and are often rare species. The tool marks and imperfect surfaces of these timbers are considered charming accents to the wood's grain and color, and the timbers are usually used as exposed beams or mantles after a light resurfacing.

SMOOTH PLANED

In some cases, you may want to focus entirely on the natural grain and color of the wood, and not the distress marks of age. Smooth-planed boards and timbers are, as the name indicates, surfaced smooth to the touch, removing all apparent imperfections and completely revealing the natural character of the wood. But even in this case, the finish may have mellowed with time, offering captivating rich color and tone. That's why the finish is often preserved on smooth-planed members.

SALVAGE WISDOM: THE QUARTER-SAWN ADVANTAGE

Not to be confused with sawing techniques that texture the face of the wood, quarter sawing is a method of cutting logs into boards. Where the more common plain sawing cuts boards out of the log in parallel layers, quarter sawing cuts boards at 90-degree angles to the growth rings, essentially in a pattern radiating out from the center. This yields fewer boards and greater waste than plain sawing does. But the grain of quarter-sawn boards is much more captivating. Straight and tight grain lines usually run the length of the board, with small "rays" and "fleck," imperfections scattered throughout the surface pattern that make for a very attractive surface look. Quarter-sawn boards are also considered better lumber, because the structure resists warping, twisting, and other distortions. The grain produced is also more water resistant, although quarter-sawn boards still take stain well.

RECLAIMED WOOD GRADES

Most companies that deal in reclaimed lumber grade the wood in their inventory. Unfortunately, grading is not standardized within the industry or even informally among resellers. However, most resellers and salvage firms break their available stock down into three general grades: a premium high-end grade, a mid-grade, and a bottom grade. The differences are a matter of visible and structural imperfections. High-end wood will feature even graining, with few if any knotholes or obvious interruptions in the grain pattern. The color will tend to be fairly uniform throughout the wood, and board to board. Mid-range lumber will have less consistent grain patterns, and the surface appearance will feature some telltale variations in color. Boards rated on the low end of the scale may have significant grain distortions and visible imperfections, and the color throughout may vary wildly, even over the span of a given board

But don't get locked into thinking that grade determines the board you should buy. Although grading will reveal, to one extent or another, the structural integrity of a piece of lumber, even lower-grade boards will hold up fine as wall paneling or flooring. As far as appearances go, it's simply not as easy as good, better, and best.

What the appearance of any given wood stock means for you depends greatly on where and how you plan on using the wood. For instance, if you are installing reclaimed flooring or paneling in a country-style home to complement a rustic look, knotty pine or wormy chestnut may be the ideal choice for you—even though they would be graded at the low end of the scale because

of all their imperfections. Flooring for a modern home would likely be far clearer "high-grade" stock.

Ultimately, it pays to inspect the wood firsthand. Grades can give you some guidance, but you should let your own goals and taste determine which you choose.

Sand back a spot of finish when you evaluate wood you are considering buying.

RECLAIMING WOOD

Before you can use reclaimed wood in any home-design project, you need to actually reclaim the wood. You may find exactly what you need—and as much as you need—at a salvage company or reclaimed building materials vendor. But the reality is, their inventories change with surprising frequency. This varying supply may mean that you have to look elsewhere for the wood you want. Or, it may just be that you want the hands-on experience of salvaging your own wood. Either way, it pays to know how to get the wood you need and prep it for the project you have in mind.

When you salvage wood from an existing building, the goal is to remove the lumber you want with minimum damage to the wood, keeping it as intact as possible. If your source is a worksite dumpster, a local dump, or a third party such as an individual who

has just completed demolishing his own garage, you'll probably need to clean and prepare the wood before you can safely and efficiently use it.

The number-one risk in using reclaimed wood is hidden metal in the lumber. Striking a sunken screw when sawing through a reclaimed 4 x 4 for a trestle table is not only disconcerting, it's also very dangerous. The other important consideration is appearance. One of the main reasons anyone chooses to use reclaimed wood is because older wood is often more attractive. Depending on what you're using the wood for, you'll have to decide if you're going to sand down the surface completely, clean the surface and stabilize the existing finish under a coat of clear sealant, or simply leave the finish as is. A lot depends on where you got the wood from and what shape it's in. If you've rescued exterior redwood siding grayed from years of exposure, and want to use it as interior wall paneling, you'll probably completely clean and seal the surface. On the other hand, reusing plank floors from a tobacco barn as new flooring in your great room may mean keeping that patina of age that was built up over decades of smoke from a curing fire. Other preparation may include cutting or ripping lumber to size for your purposes, or otherwise sawing to the dimensions and lengths you need.

But no matter what you do to the wood, it's wise to exploit as much of the innate beauty of the material as possible. If you're going to the extra effort to use reclaimed wood, you might as well use it in a way that best showcases the unique aspects of older lumber.

An easy way to check what type of wood has been painted over when reclaiming materials from a structure is to pry up a sample and look at the ends or back.

RECLAIMING WOOD SIDING

The siding on older buildings is one of the best sources for reclaimed wood. The planks are usually long and plentiful enough to supply all the wood you'll need for just about any purpose you can dream up. If the siding was correctly installed, chances are that the lumber is structurally in good shape (although you may be faced with the occasional warped or cracked plank).

The process of reclaiming wood siding is a fairly simple one, especially if the interior walls are not clad. But even if they are, you simply remove the interior walls with a hammer and pry bar, as well as any insulation lining the wall cavities (do not handle asbestos or urea formaldehyde insulation yourself—they require professional abatement and disposal). Once you have access to the inside of the siding, removing it is just a matter of some careful hammering and prying.

Start by rapping the topmost board as close as possible to where it attaches to a stud. Hit only as hard as necessary to work the nails out, but not hard enough to crack the wood. Hammer until the siding board releases from the stud. Move outside and deliver a quick, sharp blow at the nail location, to slam the siding back down against the stud and free the nails. If you can't easily hammer the siding away from the stud without cracking the wood, use a pry bar to work the plank away from the framing. Remove nails as you work and use a helper to hold up the plank once you get to the last set of nails.

When you remove a board, check it for any nails that might have been left in it. Stack the siding in a convenient location, using bolsters every few feet of length to separate layers and protect against damage.

A pry bar can be a big help in removing siding that is held by stubborn nails. Use steady, even force rather than quick and hard levering. Exercise patience and the siding will eventually come free without cracking or other damage.

DENAILING RECLAIMED LUMBER

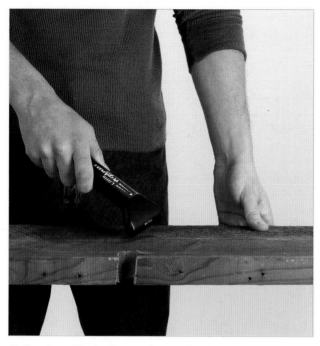

Finding the nail is the first step in removing it. That's why a handheld metal detector is a must for checking reclaimed lumber. A hidden nail or screw can destroy a saw blade and cause serious injury to the operator.

Nippers are a good choice for removing nails carefully, to limit damage to the board face. However, they will not work on sunken nails or flush nail heads because the pinchers need room to close over the nail body to pull it out.

Extractor pulling pliers are specifically designed for maximum leverage. They are quite effective for removing nails and other fasteners with a minimum of damage to the face of the wood. They are also easy and quick to use, but less effective on stubborn nails in hardwood.

Use a cat's paw for large, stubborn, embedded nails. Tap the slot of the tool under the nail head by rapping on it with a hammer. Pull back on the handle. Use a scrap of wood under the cat's paw head for extra leverage. A cat's paw is a blunt instrument and a last recourse, usually reserved for rough or hand-hewn timbers because it will likely mar the surface.

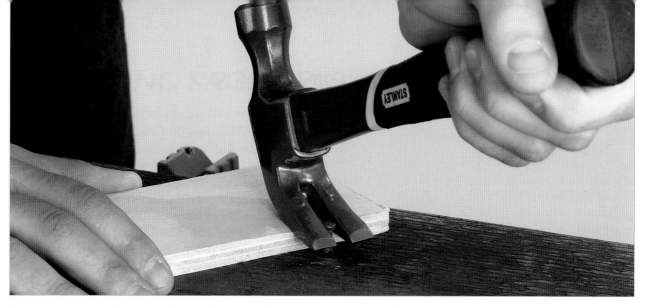

The time-tested method of prying nails out with the claw of a claw hammer works as effectively with reclaimed wood as it does with new lumber. Use a scrap of plywood or other soft pad under the head of the hammer to increase leverage and protect the face of the wood.

SEPARATING LAMINATED LUMBER

Separating laminated members is often necessary to salvage pieces for reuse. For instance, delaminating a header of sandwiched 2 x 8s can yield all the usable wood you'll need for a table. Pry laminated pieces apart with long pry or crow bars, by simultaneously pushing and pulling to create separation. Separating larger laminated sections will be easier with two people, providing extra muscle to force the pry bars in opposite directions.

SALVAGE WISDOM: MANAGING MOISTURE CONTENT

Moisture is an issue with reclaimed wood just as it is with any other type of lumber. Luckily, most reclaimed wood has had a long time to dry out. Unless the wood has been left outside in extremely wet conditions, it should be fine for immediate use. If you suspect that it has been overexposed to moisture—especially if you're salvaging the wood yourself—it's wise to check the wood with a moisture meter before using it in a final installation. In most cases, you want the wood to register under 10 percent moisture, but the drier the better. It's also smart to acclimate reclaimed wood in the final space before installing it as a matter of course. Leave it in the space for several days to a week before using it, to help the wood adjust to the exact moisture levels and temperature within that space.

knife as wide as practical for the wood surface. Using a heat gun takes a bit of practice, because if the paint isn't hard enough, you'll have to put a lot of effort into scraping with the putty knife and you risk gouging the wood. Too much heat, though, can make the paint overly sticky and gummy, making it difficult to gather and remove from the knife. A heat gun should never be used on paint containing lead, because the heated paint will release lead fumes.

CHEMICAL STRIPPING

There are many different types of chemical strippers, but most are extremely toxic. Newer types, including soy-based formulas, are less so, but safer strippers tend to work more slowly and are somewhat less effective for stubborn paint. In any case, check labels for required safety precautions and ventilation requirements. The strippers are either paste or liquids, although paste strippers are easier to handle and apply. They are applied following the manufacturer's directions, but most are brushed on, allowed to sit, and then scraped off with a putty knife or other scraping tool. Wood covered in several layers of paint often requires more than one application of stripper. Using a chemical paint stripper is a messy job, so be sure to set up an adequate work area.

SCRAPING AND SANDING

Sometimes the quickest and most efficient method of removing paint—not to mention other surface finishes—is by sanding and scraping it off. This is especially true on flat, unadorned surfaces. Painted wood surfaces are usually scraped for repainting rather than to remove all the paint. Scrapers come in a variety of shapes and sizes, from wide flat types, to tiny V-shaped scrapers for cleaning out grooves and other woodworking details. Sanding a painted surface is a more complete option that usually entails removing everything down to bare wood. A properly sanded wood surface can be repainted, stained, or refinished natural. Light sanding may be all that is necessary to prepare a surface for a new coat of paint. As with scrapers, there are specialized sanding tools for the nooks and crannies of casework, cabinetry, furniture, or molding. These include sanding cords that are like twine made of sandpaper, and oval sanding blocks for getting inside curved wood pieces.

Chemical paint strippers can be effective, but they need to be applied liberally for best results. If the wood is covered by only one or two coats of paint, you may be able to remove the paint down to the wood surface in one pass. Where the wood has been painted in many layers, you'll most likely need more than one application.

Specialized scrapers are ideal for removing loose paint and quickly preparing a simple reclaimed wood structure—such as wood window frame or vintage casework—for repainting.

RECLAIMED WOOD REPAIRS

When it comes to using reclaimed wood, whether it's flooring, an antique panel door, cabinetry, or some other type, there is a fine line between interesting and attractive surface imperfections and ugly, structurally compromising damage. Getting the most out of salvaged wood means being able to assess and fix any problems that fall on the wrong side of that line.

ROT

The wood reclaimed from older buildings may have been exposed to the elements or adverse conditions for a very long time. That's why inspecting any vintage wood for rot is a key part of the reuse process. Probe suspect sections with an awl to determine if rot has established within the wood. Often though, rotted wood sections will be quite apparent to the naked eye. In some cases, such as antique paneling or casework, rehabilitating the piece will entail cleaning out the rot and sanding or chiseling down to stable wood. Working with a flat surface such as plank flooring or siding, cross-cut the surface back from the rotted edge.

Certain situations, such as salvaged casework with rot at the bottom, or a plank that has rotted along the edge near the center of its length, may call for the more creative solution. There are a number of "wood consolidation" products on the market. These are usually two-part epoxies, mixed together to form an infiltrating liquid that is poured or brushed over the rotted surface. The liquid penetrates the rot and dries to form a solid structure that can be sanded or formed with a surform tool, file, sandpaper, or other implement. If the rot has eroded sections of the wood, the consolidation mixture can be used as primer for an adhesive wood putty. The putty is also a two-part formulation—a resin paste that is mixed with a hardener. The putty is applied with a putty knife to replicate the missing section of wood, and then allowed to dry. When it's dry it is sanded to match the profile of the surrounding wood. The wood is usually painted after epoxy consolidators or wood putty have been used, unless the rotted section was small or will be hidden from view—in which case the wood can be stained or finished natural.

DENTS

Dents in a wood surface are not charming indications of age like some scars or worm holes. Fortunately, you can easily remove dents, even in a finished wood surface. Moisten a clean, white cloth with distilled water, and place it over the dent. Lightly touch the dent area with the tip of a hot iron and the dent should come out. Deeper dents need to be filled with wood putty. Use tintable wood putty and tint it to a shade to match the wood species or existing finish. If the dent is in a noticeable area, you may want to spend some time with different color tints and a small paint brush, and re-create the grain pattern over the dent.

GOUGES, NAIL AND SCREW HOLES

Whether you leave or repair scratches or holes in a wood surface is largely a matter of the look you're after. If you want a distressed, antique appearance, chances are you'll leave many of these small imperfections. However, if you're using the wood specifically for the grain and appearance of the species, you'll probably want to repair many, if not all, of the modest blemishes in the surface. Use sandable wood filler to fix these surface flaws. You can purchase tintable fillers that will allow you to add color and help the substance blend into the surface, or choose a pre-tinted filler. They are available in a range of shades to match different wood tones. Press the filler into the gouge or hole, level it off, and allow it dry. Then lightly sand the surface to complete the repair.

Nail holes, gouges, dents, and scratches often can be fixed with just a little bit of tinted wood putty.

SALVAGE WISDOM: FOOTWEAR FOR SALVAGED DOORS

Rot, especially rot along an unfinished bottom edge, is a common problem with antique doors. Left untreated, the rot can spread. Solve the problem by removing the rotted portion and cladding the bottom of the door in a protective metal "shoe." Mark the cut line right above the rot, snapping a chalk line across the door face. Use a straightedge clamped to the door and positioned so that the circular saw blade cuts along the cut line. Sand and seal the cut edge, and cut the shoe—available at home centers and hardware stores—to the width of the door. Screw the shoe onto the bottom edge and install the door in its opening.

RECLAIMED WOOD FLOORING

A home's flooring is all about beauty and comfort underfoot. No flooring is more beautiful and comfortable than wood, and no wood brings a more unique character to your home than a reclaimed wood floor. Once you begin looking for just the right reclaimed wood, you'll inevitably realize that the biggest challenge is narrowing down the amazing number of choices to find the best look for your home.

Old houses and other buildings yield a wealth of wood flooring that can be brought back to life in your home. These include the standard strip flooring harvested from more recent buildings being deconstructed, the plank flooring common to older buildings, more unusual pegged floors (which require special techniques to salvage and re-lay), and even end grain flooring, a tile-type of floor using "bricks" of wood. But older buildings also provide other elements, such as siding and paneling, which can be repurposed as new wood flooring. Even beams and other timbers can be milled to serve as flooring. You simply won't find a larger selection of potential species, styles, and looks for a floor than among reclaimed wood.

There are two ways to get the flooring material you want in the amount you need. The first is to go to the source. Wood flooring is one of the easiest elements to salvage from a building. Removing elements like flooring during deconstruction is called "soft-stripping" for just that reason. Unlike structural members, flooring can be removed with relatively little expertise or effort. Even if you're faced with converting square-cut siding or paneling to your purposes, you can turn it into flooring by milling your own tongue and grooves into the boards. Certainly, this is a lot of work and requires the right tools and attention to detail. But do-it-yourself milling can save you enormous amounts of money.

However, you may simply prefer to go the easier route and purchase reclaimed flooring in quantity from any of a number of salvage firms and companies that deal in reclaimed wood. Consider available stock carefully. Not only do you need to ensure that the amount of a given flooring available through the supplier is sufficient for your needs, you also need to know the flooring you buy is fairly consistent board to board. In most cases, the company will have removed all the boards as part of a single salvage project, so the boards were already fit together as a floor. Sometimes, a bit of mixing and matching does occur. But for the most part, suppliers will have grouped like boards, and

Reclaimed barn siding was lightly sanded before being installed for the floor in this stunning bedroom. The color variations in the floor planks provide endless fascination and integrate perfectly with the exposed beams and wood ceiling.

many even pre-finish the boards, making installation even easier.

Generally, you'll use the same process to install a reclaimed wood floor as you would a new wood floor. However, some techniques may differ, depending on the type of flooring you've chosen. For instance, if you're installing an aged, exceptionally wide plank floor, you may need to face-nail—and plug over the face nails—to ensure against cupping or warping. The same is true if you've reclaimed a pegged wood floor and are re-creating that distinctive look in your new home. Complete the installation with the finish of your choice, whether you're leaving the existing surface largely intact, or completely sanding down and refinishing it.

RECLAIMING A VINTAGE WOOD FLOOR

Reclaiming some wood building materials directly from an existing structure can be a challenge. Structural members such as timbers and beams must be extracted carefully to prevent wholesale collapse. Others, such as siding, are arduous to remove and will need exceptional amounts of prep to be reused. But wood flooring is one of the easiest and most rewarding materials to salvage. Do it right, and you may not even need to refinish the reclaimed flooring after you re-install it.

The process is fairly straightforward and is basically the reverse of installing a wood floor. Start by clearing the room you're working in and remove shoe or other base moldings. Remove the first and possibly second row of boards on the tongue side of the floor. This may require destroying one or more boards to gain access.

Do that by using a pry bar on damaged flooring, or a circular saw and pry bar, to cut into and tear out boards so that you have clear access for prying out the adjacent rows.

Removing planks from that point is relatively easy. Slide the tongue of a pry bar under the tongue of the plank next to a nail, and pry the nail up. Do this at each nail location until the plank is completely loose. Then pry up and toward you to release it from the next row. Continue removing planks, taking care not to damage the tongues as you remove the boards. Remove all the nails as you work, and check boards for nails before finally placing them neatly in stacks separated by bolsters.

Stack reclaimed flooring neatly, well supported by bolsters. If you are planning on using the flooring with its existing finish intact, separate the layers with building paper.

SALVAGE WISDOM: ACCLIMATING RECLAIMED FLOORS

Wood planks or strips that you reclaim should already be thoroughly dry, because they have likely been inside for decades. However, in some cases you will have rescued the wood from a dilapidated building so far gone that the floors were exposed to the elements for quite a while. In other cases, resellers may have stored reclaimed wood flooring outside. Wood flooring in these situations can absorb moisture. But even if it's just a matter of temperature change, you need to give the flooring a chance to adjust to its new environment. That's why, just as you would with new wood flooring, you should store reclaimed wood planks, strips or end grain tiles in the room where they will ultimately be installed for at least 24 hours prior to installation.

MILLING TONGUES AND GROOVES INTO RECLAIMED PLANKS

1 Joint one edge of each plank using a jointer. If you don't have a jointer, you can joint the edge using a table saw with a jointer jig. A properly jointed edge will be necessary for the boards to fit snugly together when laid as a floor.

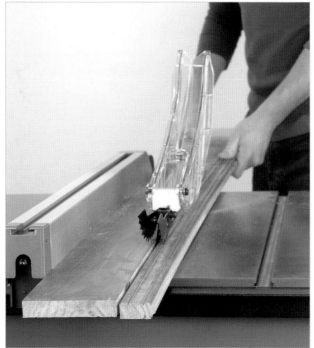

2 Use your table saw to rip the opposite edge of each board so that it is perfectly parallel to the jointed edge.

3 Saw the grooves first. Set a dado blade to the appropriate height, and set the table saw fence so that the groove runs along the middle of the edge. Stack dado blades as necessary to cut wider grooves in thicker stock. Cut the first groove in a test piece.

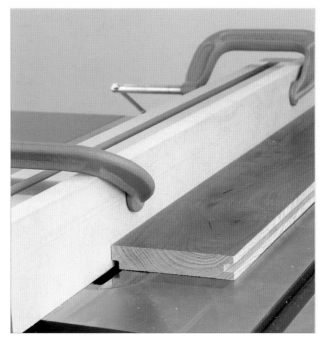

4 Reset the fence to cut the tongues. Use a short or scrap piece to cut the first tongue. Err on the side of cutting tongues too thick, because you can always cut more off, but you'll be in trouble if the tongues do not fit snugly.

(Continued)

5 Check the fit of the tongue into the groove, with both pieces laying flat. The fit should be snug enough that you have to apply some force to join the two pieces.

6 Once you're certain that the measurements are all correct, cut all the grooves first. Check each for fit, using the tongue on the scrap piece. Finally, cut all the tongues on the other edges of the planks.

7 Check all the planks one last time, paying special attention to any burrs or imperfections in the tongues and grooves. Sand down any spots that might prove troublesome when installing the floor.

ROUTING TONGUE-AND-GROOVE FLOORING

Routing tongues and grooves into wood planks is a great alternative to cutting them with a table saw. The routing is done with special adjustable tongue-and-groove router bits—one for each function (shown at right). The directions here describe using a router table, although you can also use a hand router with a special jig. The router table, however, is much quicker and easier (and safer) to use. Prepare the planks for routing by jointing and ripping them.

1 Set the groove bit into the router and cut a groove. Swap the bits and cut a tongue on a sacrificial piece. Check that the tongue and groove fit snugly together, and that the companion pieces sit flat when connected.

2 Replace the groove bit and rout all the grooves first. Swap bits and rout all the tongues. Check that the tongues and grooves are all clean. Sand as necessary to fix any imperfections.

LAYING TONGUE-AND-GROOVE RECLAIMED PLANK FLOORING

Perhaps the most common use for reclaimed wood is as flooring. And the most common type of reclaimed floor is a wide plank floor. In fact, the planks can be as wide as 10 inches. Although this means that the planks can be a little more cumbersome to handle than modern hardwood strip flooring, take heart: wide plank floors go down much quicker than their strip counterparts.

The look of a wide plank floor is impressive. It can make a space seem larger and a plank floor can visually anchor the room. Keep in mind that each plank presents much more visual area than a strip would. An oddly colored or patterned strip over the span of a wood floor would hardly get noticed; in a plank floor, an odd duck will stick out like a sore thumb. You can minimize the impact any unusual-looking plank has on the floor's overall appearance by shuffling it to an outside edge of the floor. If you're lucky, you may even need to rip it down to fit, minimizing its impact even more.

The finish you choose may affect how you work with the wood during installation. If you're planning on sanding and refinishing the floor entirely, you can proceed to work as quickly and efficiently as possible. However, if you've chosen your planks for their historical finish, you'll want to work with soft gloves and be as careful with tools, such as power nailers, which sit right on the surface of planks. Also be careful in moving planks around as you pull them off the stack. Any noticeable scratches will proably rule out keeping the vintage finish.

Lastly, it's a good idea to face-nail and plug wide planks if they were previously pegged, or if you expect that the space will experience regular variations in temperature. A cupped or warping plank floor will not be the showcase for which you chose reclaimed wood in the first place.

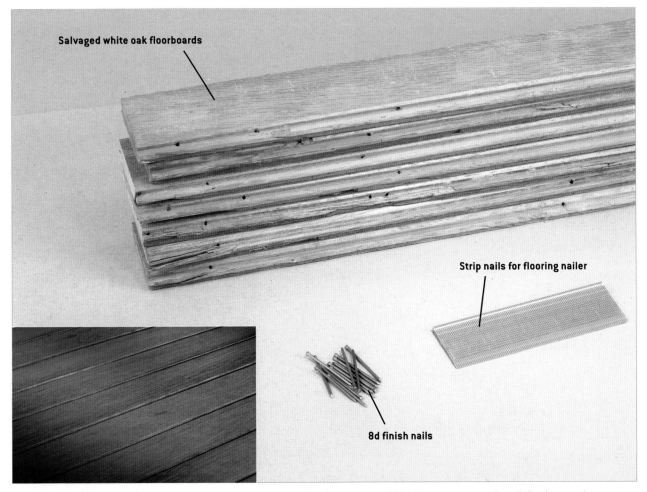

Salvaged white oak floorboards

Strip nails for flooring nailer

8d finish nails

Salvaged floorboards come in varieties and sizes that can be hard to find in new material, like the quartersawn white oak flooring seen here. Sanded and finished it has a rich color (inset).

1 Measure the room and double-check that you have all the planks you'll need to cover the surface and account for waste. Make sure the subfloor is clean and free of loose nails or other debris. If the boards have a distinctive pattern or coloration that will affect positioning, decide on the positions and number the planks.

2 Roll underlayment out to cover the subfloor surface. Staple it to the subfloor with a staple gun. Overlap each strip by several inches, and cut as necessary with a utility knife equipped with a new blade.

3 Locate floor joists, nail a brad at each end, and snap chalk lines over the centerline of each floor joist. Nail and snap another chalk line perpendicular to these lines, between 1/4" and 1/2" from the edge of the starting wall.

4 Drill pilot holes every 8" to 10" along the length of the planks that you'll use as a starter row. Drill the holes in the face, along the inside groove edge that will face the wall. This is to prevent any cracking or damage during face-nailing of the first row.

(Continued)

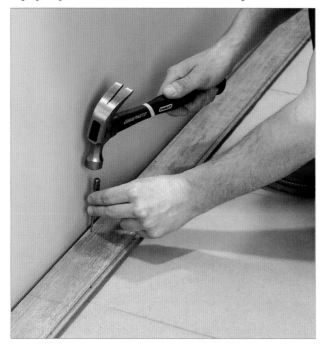

5 Ensure that the first plank is properly positioned with its inside edge along the starter chalk line. Hammer finish nails through the pilot holes, until the heads are just above the surface. Sink the nails using a nailset.

6 Drill pilot holes in the first plank's tongue, every 8" to 10" along its length. Drill at a 45° angle into the joist locations. Blind nail a finish nail into each hole, and use a nailset to sink it.

7 Snug new rows in place with a scrap piece (milled with a groove slightly larger than the tongues on your planks) set against the tongue. Tap the piece lightly with a wood mallet until the new plank is tight against the existing row.

8 After the first row, nail planks into place with a power nailer. Position the lip over the edge of the plank, and hit the strike button with a rubber mallet.

9 Stagger the planks to create a brickwork pattern. Cut planks face up, using a miter saw equipped with an 80-tooth blade. Saw end planks so that the cut end will face the wall.

10 If you encounter a plank that is bowed or warped and won't easily snug up to the preceding row, make a wedge from a scrap 2 x 4 by sawing diagonally from one corner to the other. Nail a 2 x 4 scrap to the floor, and tap the wedge into position to force the plank into place for nailing.

11 Rip final-row planks to the width necessary to fit them between the next-to-last row of planks and the wall, leaving an expansion gap of between 1/4" and 1/2". Pull the plank into place with a pry bar, and then face-nail using the same process you used on the first row.

12 Sand and finish the floor as desired, or leave a pre-finished or distressed surface as is. Stain or finish shoe molding as necessary, and nail it into place around perimeter of room.

SALVAGING PEGGED PLANK FLOORING

1 Remove the first two rows of planks, as you would to begin reclaiming any wood flooring. Using a spade bit one size smaller than the pegging plugs, drill out the plugs in the face of the boards, exposing the face nails.

2 Slip the point of the wrecker's adze under the edge of the board at the position of one set of face nails. Tap the butt of the adze lightly with a hammer to wedge the adze under the plank. Lever the handle back and forth to loosen the face nails, tapping the adze further under the board as necessary. Continue working the handle until the plank under it can be pulled free without causing damage to the wood.

LAYING PEGGED PLANK FLOORING

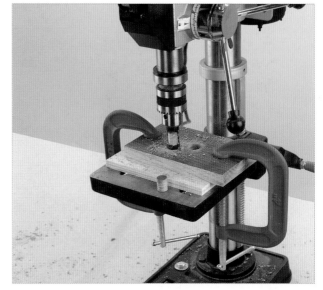

1 Lay the flooring as described on pages 53-55. Clean out the peg holes with a small chisel, and hammer 8d finish nails through the holes in the face. If you want to add the peg look to plain plank flooring without face nailing you can also use a spade bit to drill peg holes in the face.

2 Once all the planks are installed, cut the pegs with a drill press fitted with a plug-cutting bit in the correct size. The plugs can be a contrasting wood, or the same wood stained a different finish. Fit the pegs in the holes after coating them with carpenter's glue. Use a pull saw to cut the plug off even with the plank's surface after the glue dries, and sand lightly until smooth.

END GRAIN FLOORS

Spend enough time searching through old industrial buildings and once-grand turn-of-the-century homes, and sooner or later you will come across the interesting and potentially gorgeous wood flooring known as *end grain flooring*. Also called "wood block" flooring, end grain floors are made of tiles cut from timber ends. Because the cuts are made across the board, the end grain is exposed on the face of the tile, just as it would be on a chopping block. And, as with chopping block, the surface of an end grain tile is incredibly tough and durable.

That durability is why the first uses for these wood block tiles were as a street paving material (and some of those streets are still in existence today), and as floors for industrial facilities. Chances are, you won't find a tougher home flooring material.

But that toughness belies an incredibly beautiful side. End-grain pattern is more intense and visually dynamic than any other wood grain, and was stained, painted, and finished natural. The look of reclaimed end grain tiles varies with the type of wood used and where the tiles were installed. Depending on the look you're after, you can refinish the tiles to create a shiny end grain floor that looks almost like polished brick, or lay a satin-finish surface with hypnotic patterns unlike any other type of flooring. You can also take advantage

of the time-seasoned appearance of your reclaimed tiles, worn as they will be from many years of foot (or tire) traffic. Not only do the tiles present a vast number of potential surface finishes, the arrangement of the tiles can be varied from a simple brick pattern, to a herringbone design, to a more random pattern. You can also leave spaces between the end grain blocks to be filled with flexible wood filler, or you can butt each tile up against the others to create a solid-surface appearance. Either way, the surface must be sealed to prevent dirt and moisture from penetrating.

The floors are laid somewhat like other tile floors, although the adhesive is different; the surface of an end-grain floor is either sealed with a clear polyurethane after cleaning and a very light sanding (if you want to keep the aged appearance) or it is sanded in much the same fashion as a hardwood strip floor is, if you're looking for a completely new surface appearance. But given the potential complexity of the floor's pattern and the work required for laying it, end grain floors are usually limited to smaller spaces and those areas that don't require complex adjustments to the pattern to accommodate built-in fixtures. Either way, an end grain floor is more difficult to install than other wood floors, requiring patience and attention to detail. The result, however, is usually well worth your trouble.

END-GRAIN TILES: CUT YOUR OWN

You don't necessarily have to purchase reclaimed end grain tiles to have a wood block floor; you can make your own. Use a bandsaw to cut inch-thick slices from a 2x6 or other piece of reclaimed lumber (such as the antique pine timber being sliced into 6" x 6" tiles).

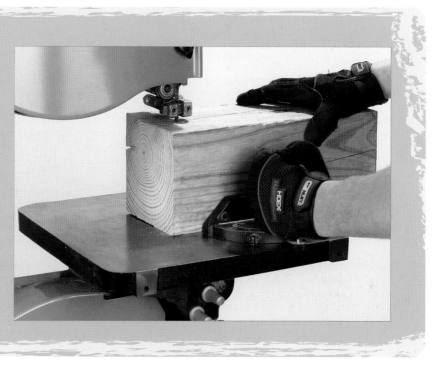

LAYING RECLAIMED END GRAIN FLOORING

1 Establish the overall tile pattern. Work the pattern out on sketch paper first, using the dimensions of the room to scale. Once you've figured out the pattern, dry lay the actual tiles to ensure that it works to your satisfaction.

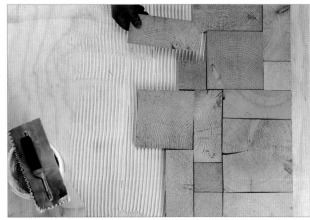

2 Snap chalk lines to divide the space into four quadrants. Lay one quadrant at a time, starting at the center. Spread a bed of polyurethane adhesive, according to the manufacturer's instructions, setting the tiles in place either butted up to one another, or using spacers to leave room for grout.

3 Cut tiles with a band saw or jig saw as necessary to fit around obstacles and at the outer edges of the design. Leave a 1/2" gap at walls, and around obstructions such as pillars, to allow for expansion. Once all the tiles are laid, let the floor set for 24 hours, or as long as recommended by the adhesive manufacturer.

4 Spread flexible, sandable flexible wood filler into large cracks in the surface of individual tiles. If you're refinishing the surface, sand with a drum sander equipped with 60-grit sandpaper. Sand across the grain to start with, and make a final pass with the grain.

✚ SAFETY FIRST

Lead paint is commonly found in older homes, most often on painted woodwork and walls. This includes wood interior and exterior doors, which may have been painted with several layers of lead paint. The first step in dealing with the issue is determining if the door you're considering was painted with lead paint. Simple test kits available from home centers and hardware stores can quickly identify any lead in a painted surface. Test for lead whenever you're reclaiming or buying a salvaged door that has been painted. You can also use the test to detect lead paint on timbers, wood shelving, flooring, and other surfaces.

RECLAIMING WOOD DOORS

Wood doors are the low-hanging fruit of reclaimed building materials. Easy to get at and just as easy to remove, these essential building elements can be plucked from just about any building or structure whose time has come to an end. More contemporary versions become available as homeowners tear down walls and reconfigure layouts and floor plans as part of major home renovations.

Whether you're interested in a set of distressed doors for your kitchen cabinets, looking for a sturdy entryway with distinctive style, or just trying to match the interior six-panel doors in your three-bedroom Victorian, you'll find a spectacular number of alternatives available through many different sources. Salvaging doors right from the source is often the most desirable option because it takes very little time and effort (you won't need much beyond a measuring tape, hammer, pry bar, screwdriver, and a half an hour). A far wider selection can be found at salvage companies. But no matter what source you use, expect to be faced with an almost overwhelming number of variables. Door styles have changed frequently through time, and many different styles were used in any given historical period.

Beyond their obvious use as new or replacement units, doors can be recycled as pieces of furniture. A basic eight-panel front entryway unit can be refinished in your favorite color, set on top of two painted sawhorses—or better yet, legs made of reclaimed staircase newels—and covered with glass to make a stunning desk. A panel door can be refinished and distressed to serve as wonderful country-style headboard for a bed. They can even be taken apart for reuse. Older doors are usually solid wood, with stunning grain patterns and coloring that can bring a handsome appearance to plain bookshelves, benches and other small projects.

But by far, the biggest reclaimed use for doors, is as doors. Some fit the current standard interior door widths of 28", 30" or 32", or the exterior standard of 36". Others, such as barn doors, are built to unique measurements and either the opening or the door will have to be modified. Some doors come pre-hung—that is to say, nested in their own door frame—but most of the doors that are reclaimed are standalone units perfect for retrofitting into an existing doorway. How much work you need to do to cut down or otherwise customize the door for your location will be an important consideration in selecting a new door. Buy a door that needs to be drastically downsized to fit your opening and you risk making the door look odd. On the other hand, you should simply never buy a door that is too small for the opening. These points are true whether you're looking for interior, exterior, or cabinet doors.

WHICH HAND?

Obviously, it's essential that you know how the door you're considering will go into the opening. Any exterior or interior door with a handle is generally categorized as either left- or right-handed. The term specifies which side the handle is on, and which side the hinges are on. If you face the door as it opens toward you, the "hand" of the door is the side the doorknob is on. Some reclaimed doors can be flipped to fit in an existing opening if necessary, while others can only be installed one way. A door's "handedness" is more important than you might imagine, because where the handle is determines which side the hinges are on, which in turn determines how the door opens. Preferably, you don't want a door to open so that the person walking through it is sandwiched between a wall and the door, or is facing a wall. Doors as a rule swing into the room you're entering or leaving. Front doors, for instance, generally open into the house.

Cabinet doors must be chosen with the same issues in mind. You need to make sure the hinges and handles are on the correct sides for the cabinets you're looking to retrofit, or that the hardware on the doors can be easily swapped without ruining the look of the doors or cabinets. Size will be another major concern if you're searching for cabinet doors, although you may be able to adapt larger doors to your purposes, if you change from face-frame or surface-mount hinges, to concealed or inset hinges. Obviously, though, no matter what type of door you're looking for, a measuring tape is your first and most essential partner in any salvage shopping trip.

RECLAIMED DOOR TYPES & STYLES

Not all doors are created equal. In fact, door styles are as varied as any architectural element. If you're adding a reclaimed interior door, it's often easiest to choose one with an identical or similar appearance to the other doors in the interior, although adding a set of French doors to a dining room or saloon doors to a kitchen can change the appearance of the room and the home. Reclaimed cabinet doors should generally all be the same. But using a reclaimed exterior door is your chance to add a focal point. Refine the look of the home with a stately walnut door containing a half-lite of beveled glass. Create a Tuscan look with an arched, board-and-batten door fitted with oversized iron hinges. The possibilities are nearly endless, but your decision begins with the types of doors available.

PANELED

This is a common style that has been used down through time for both exterior and interior openings. Different types and arrangements of panels indicate different periods in history, although most panel designs can be adapted to many different types of architecture. The doors are crafted of rail-and-stile frames, with panels that are either flush (flat), recessed, or raised. Flat-panel doors are the plainest and more commonly used as interior than exterior doors. Raised-panel doors offer the most ornamental appearance, and come in a wide variety of panel configurations. The same is true of recessed-panel doors. But recessed panels appear somewhat less ornate and plainer than raised-panel doors do.

This six-panel interior door is made of fir, but it blends well with the reclaimed oak casing.

Wood panel doors are becoming very rare for exterior locations because they are not as efficient as non-wood doors and are more prone to movement and warpage.

SALVAGE WISDOM: COMMON DOOR PANEL STYLES

Horizontal Raised Panels

This look is strongly identified with the Prairie school and craftsman design movements, and is best suited for modern house styles. The doors usually feature four, five, or six horizontal panels stacked between the stiles. The look is subdued but pleasing.

Eight-panel Colonial

Although not distinctively different from some Victorian and contemporary doors, the colonial style was defined by alternating square and rectangular vertical panels. The look is extremely adaptable and is used in many different home styles.

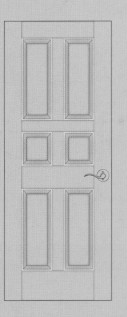

Six-panel Victorian

The configuration of Victorian panel doors differed from earlier and later versions in subtle but noticeable ways. Panels were often stacked at irregular distances, as this example shows. Victorian-era door panels were also much more likely to be arched.

Four-panel Traditional

This configuration, or others similar to it, has been in use from the mid-20th century through to the present. It's a visually pleasing if un-complicated arrangement of two panel pairs, one larger than the other.

BOARD-AND-BATTEN

Think old west, country, or rural. This is the most rustic style of door, with vertical boards forming the body of the door, and battens run horizontally and/or diagonally to hold the whole thing together. This is a very distinctive style, appropriate for a limited number of home styles. The doors look odd when painted, so you have to accept the country appeal on its own merits. Arched versions are more "wine-country" than "back country," but still would not look right on most contemporary, traditional or modern structures. Style aside, the insulating value is very low. However, the right board-and-batten door can add to the charm of a cottage or a summer home, and they make excellent doors for fences bordering flower gardens or other well-landscaped yards.

FRENCH DOORS

Dating from the 17th century, French doors were common enough throughout history that they now make regular appearances as part of salvage companies' inventories. The original idea behind the French door was to let light pass freely throughout the living space. Although they still serve that function today, you'd be wiser to use reclaimed French doors on the interior, because the single panes don't have the insulation value that a more solid door does. All French doors feature top-to-bottom glass, but the number and arrangement of panes create a remarkable assortment of styles. Typically, the more panes, the more sophisticated the look. But more panes are also harder to keep clean—a point worthy of consideration when choosing among reclaimed French doors. The doors are used both as single and double doors, although the most impressive use is as a set, for instance in the entryway to a formal dining room. A single French door with a grid of lites can also be turned into a rather stunning table or desk. Or mount one on the wall, filling each pane with a different picture, to make a visually captivating photographic montage.

PANEL-LITE

Putting a window in an otherwise solid door has long been a way to let the sunlight into a home and take advantage of a view (or keep an eye out for visitors). Panel "lites"—the term used for panes of glass in doors and adjacent areas—come in as many shapes and sizes as solid-panel doors do. Exterior doors most often have glass in the top half of the door, and the lite is frequently made of art glass. Using beveled, machined, or stained glass in a door's half lite allows sunlight to

penetrate, but obscures the view to maintain privacy. Other styles of glass, such as a fan lite at the top of the door, are indicative of certain styles and particular to certain tastes.

CABINET DOORS

New cabinet doors can give the whole kitchen a face-lift, and reclaimed cabinet doors come in as many different styles as their contemporary counterparts. They're also an inexpensive alternative to replacing or refacing your existing cabinets. Cabinet doors come in flat, raised-panel, and recessed-panel profiles, as well as versions with glass inserts either divided or undivided by muntins. Glass inserts can be frosted, beveled, machined, or plain glass, all of which can bring a distinctive look to the kitchen. Selecting the right salvaged cabinet doors can be a bit of a challenge. You have to find a size that will work, a style that suits your taste, and enough doors for all your cabinets. However, the cost will likely be a bargain, and you can often get great impact out of just replacing upper or lower cabinet doors.

BI-FOLD AND CLOSET DOORS

Upgrade a room's look with a nice set of vintage closet doors, or make long bookshelves out of disassembled solid-wood bi-fold doors. Louvered, solid, and glass folding doors are all commonly reclaimed from older homes, and newer remodels. Stripping and staining solid-wood closet doors can be a great way to add some style to a bedroom, while painting louvered doors in vivid colors can be a excellent way to jazz up an otherwise boring area of any room.

POCKET DOORS

These space savers have been around since Victorian times, and they are still fashionable and ideal for tight rooms. Salvaged pocket doors include those that look like French doors, simple solid versions, and panel doors. It's possible that you may be able to convert a pocket door into a hinged door, although they are often too short for standard openings. If you plan on re-using a pocket door you've reclaimed, make sure the tracks are in good shape. Track quality has varied over time, and track failure can lead to a lot of frustration. If you have doubts about the tracks that come with the door, look to replace them with newer hardware.

HANGING A RECLAIMED DOOR IN AN EXISTING JAMB

Adapting a door, especially an antique door, to an existing opening can be tricky. The older the door, the more likely it is to be an unusual size and the greater the chance that the door will be out of true. Doors are inevitably used in high-traffic areas that stress the wood and structure on an almost constant basis. Doors get slammed, we run things into them, and gravity is forever pulling a door away from its mountings. Add to that the fact that exterior doors are subject to the elements, and it's almost amazing that there are actually older doors from which to choose.

But there are, and they can be magnificent. A vintage door may have unusual panel configurations, exceptional glass treatments, or a spectacular aged finish. Any of these can add a truly unique look to the home, in or out.

Unfortunately, they are subject to another consideration after you get them home—actually fitting inside the opening. It's not just a matter of size, although that's the key issue. The problem is, the opening itself is affected by the same stresses that plague a door. Houses settle and shift. Water damage and physical abuse from day-to-day wear and tear take their toll, and eventually any opening can become distorted to one degree or another.

That's why we've used the most accommodating way to mount an old door in a newer opening for the project that follows. The process outlined is designed to remove the least amount of door material, maintaining the character and style as much as possible. It's also an easy process to follow—you don't have to be an accomplished woodworker to achieve a solidly executed, easy-to-open retrofit. You should have, however, a helper, who will make the work much easier and less frustrating to do. Old, solid wood doors can be heavy, and trying to stabilize one while taking measurements or lining up a hinge can be a real challenge. A couple extra hands can make all the difference.

Before

After

1 Use a helper to hold the door against the jamb from the inside. Shim the bottom of the door approximately 1/2" so that the door is level with the jamb, not the floor. Center the door in the opening.

2 Mark the top and side cut lines on the door, along the inside edge of the doorframe. Mark the front of the door with colored masking tape.

3 Lay the door across sawhorses, or on a flat, level work surface with the tape side facing up. Use a pencil compass and straightedge to transfer the cut lines on the front of the door to the back (adjust the compass for several points along the line to make equivalent reference points on the back). Then scribe the lines, front and back, with a utility knife and a straightedge.

4 Trim the top of the door with a circular saw equipped with a fine-cutting blade. Use a clamped straightedge to guide the saw base, and keep the cut 1/16" on the waste side. If the edges of the door need more than 1/4" removed, trim the edges in the same way.

(Continued)

5 Use a power or hand plane to plane down all the edges to the actual cut line. Set the door in position to check fit, and plane more as needed. Use a file or sandpaper to bevel the cut edges slightly to prevent splintering.

6 Position the door in the opening and mark the hinge locations. Use a combination square to outline the new hinge mortise on the door edge. This may entail enlarging an existing mortise. Score the edges of the new mortise or modified outline with a utility knife and use a sharp chisel and hammer to modify or cut the new hinge mortise.

Option: If an existing hinge mortise overlaps the new mortise, the existing mortise may be too deep, creating an uneven bed for the hinge leaf. In this case, you'll need to install cardboard or scrap wood shims under the edge of the hinge leaf that overlaps onto the deeper, older mortise.

7 Screw the hinges into place on the door and hang the door by having a helper tip it into position against the door jamb so that the top hinge leaf sits in the top jamb mortise. Drive one screw into this leaf, then set the other hinge leaves into place and install all the remaining screws.

8 If you are using the reclaimed door's lockset, or one that fits its holes, chisel a new strikeplate mortise or modify the existing mortise to take the new strikeplate. Install the lockset and strikeplate.

SALVAGE WISDOM: RECLAIMING VS. BUYING OLD TIMBERS

Salvaging structural timbers from older buildings is not a small undertaking. Because these often support key parts of the building, removing them poses the risk of unwanted destruction of the structure and danger of serious injury. Usually, the job requires expertise beyond the skills of a home do-it-yourselfer. Even after it has been removed, moving and handling a large timber is no easy feat. However, many salvage companies around the country carry a healthy selection of reclaimed structural timbers. Depending on the company, the timber may be sold as it was salvaged—requiring that you do cleaning and any surfacing. More often, the company will have prepped the timber to one degree or another, making it ready for refinishing and use. In any case, you should be certain that you know where the timber came from and can determine what contaminants, if any, it might have been exposed to. You should also buy from a reputable salvage company. At the very least, the company should have checked the timber for fatal structural flaws and hidden metal. But the best companies kiln dry the timbers they salvage, insuring against any insect infestation and adding to the structural integrity of the piece.

WORKING WITH RECLAIMED TIMBERS & BEAMS

Structural timbers and beams are some of the most dramatic examples of reclaimed wood. Timbers are steeped in history because reclaimed structural members are usually some of the oldest wood you'll find. Big and substantial, they have an impressive physical presence. Their impact is made even more powerful by exceptional variations in surface texture. Evidence of hand crafting is one of the key allures to using reclaimed wood, and few pieces bear the marks of a craftsman's tools and expertise as blatantly as salvaged timbers and beams do. Many were hand hewn with axe, adze, and hand plane, creating a rough and unique surface full of character.

But even beams and posts that were milled with industrial saws retain arresting surface textures. Because most served purely structural and functional roles, it was considered a waste of time to plane or sand down to a perfectly smooth surface. Thick beams, timbers, and posts consequently often have a rough sawn surface, or may exhibit the scars of circle or skip sawing. Each piece has a vivid historical tale written on its surface.

As charming as they are though, these rough, crude surfaces tend to collect dirt and grime, especially in exposed locations and over the long periods of service they've commonly seen. Given all the collected grunge, using one of these members in an interior design project usually means thoroughly cleaning it first. Once you get down to a stable wood surface, you'll need to make a decision about what kind of appearance you ultimately want. Most people look to strike a balance between a timber surface that is pleasant to the touch and the eye, and one that retains the wood's original character, beauty, and woodworking marks. Depending on how the timber was manufactured in the first place, and how hard the years have been on it, reviving the wood for reuse in home design can range from a simple cleaning and light sanding to a full-scale planing and smoothing.

How fully you finish the surface depends in no small part on exactly what you have in mind for the piece. Because vintage timbers and beams are so sturdy and inherently sound, they are often incorporated into homes as exposed beams or support columns—either as purely decorative elements or actual structural members. But there are many other uses for these unique pieces. Timbers, posts, or beams of any sort make showstopping fireplace mantels, especially when

A reclaimed thick eucalyptus plank is a more appropriate mantel for this modern fireplace than a rough-cut full-scale timber would have been.

fronting a stone fireplace surround. They also work well over more contemporary steel or brick-fronted fireplaces as a contrasting design element that calls attention to its own imperfections. In any case, the timber can be centered over the fireplace, or a longer member can be used to create an asymmetrical look as attractive as it is unusual.

Timbers and beams can serve a home design in many other ways as well. Sturdy headers can be turned into wonderful wall-mounted shelves. Barn or warehouse posts can be ganged to create a fascinating room divider, or split to make unusual handrails around a deck. And the wood can be reused in a functional way by cutting and fitting it to build a trestle table or countertop. But no matter how you reuse the piece, a salvaged timber is inevitably home-design gold.

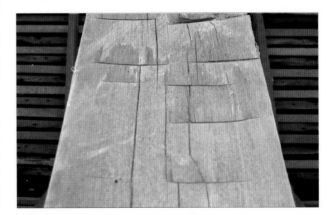

The interesting character of many reclaimed timbers lies in the marks of hand-hewn surfaces.

RESURFACING SALVAGED TIMBERS

A power washer is the quickest way to remove decades of grime and reveal the true nature of the wood below. Use a medium nozzle and pressure to quickly remove dirt and grime without damaging the wood surface. Hold the nozzle at an angle to the wood face, about 6" to 8" from the surface, and keep the spray moving.

If you want a very smooth and level surface, you may need to plane the timber. Adjust the blade on the hand planer with the adjusting knob, starting out with a shallow setting. Be sure to check for nails or screws first. Press down slightly on the front at the start of the pass, and on the back at the end, using a smooth, even stroke. Check the shavings to ensure you are taking off very little wood in an even layer.

A power planer can make quick work of an extremely rough timber surface. Start with the blades adjusted to the shallowest setting. Set the planer's front shoe on the surface, start the planer and let it get up to full speed. Then guide the planer forward. Maintain easy pressure and control the planer to keep it level at the end of the stroke and to avoid taking a chunk out of an edge.

For the smoothest surface possible, you can sand the timber. Even with a belt or palm sander, this is a tremendous amount of work. Sanding is usually only required for specialized finishes or if the timber will be used as a high-exposure surface in the home.

REVIVING VINTAGE CABINETRY

You never have too much storage. That reality was as true in years gone by as it is today, which is why you'll find a large selection of wood cabinets in salvage shops and yards. Depending on how old they are, these salvaged units are often unique wood species, with wonderful period features such as tip-out bins and spice rack drawers. Unlike modern particleboard versions, most older cabinets—and any that date back before the 1950s—are solid-wood construction. This construction is key to their longevity.

Like other reclaimed materials, cabinetry often represents a good bargain. The biggest costs—the materials and craftsmanship—have already been accounted for by the original owner. But a bargain is only a bargain if you can really make use of what you're buying. When it comes to reclaimed cabinetry, planning a whole kitchen remodel may be overreaching. It's unlikely that you'll find exactly the number and size of cabinets that fit your space. In addition, cabinet styles of decades past differ from contemporary styles. For instance, most modern kitchens incorporate recessed kickboards under bottom cabinets and leave an open space above top-mounted units, whereas the carcasses of older cabinetry often ran to the floor or all the way to the ceiling. You can modify reclaimed cabinets for your purposes, or take the easier route and use salvaged cabinets as focal points for a kitchen or dining room, or simply incorporate them into work areas as handsome utility cabinets.

In any case, you'll probably have to do some amount of refurbishing to any older cabinet you purchase. This can range from simply cleaning the unit thoroughly, to refinishing, to correcting more serious structural problems. Whatever work needs to be done, it's always easier to do it before you mount the cabinet.

You can start with the finish. As with other types of reclaimed wood, you may want to stabilize and preserve the existing finish. If the cabinet is painted, it's probably worth sanding down a small inconspicuous section underneath or inside the cabinet to determine if the wood is unique enough to merit refinishing natural. However, painted cabinets are often sanded lightly to remove loose paint and sprayed with a polyurethane sealer to fix the surface and give the cabinets an attractive distressed look. Other finishes can be removed to allow for a brand look.

Before you work on the finish of the cabinet, however, you should thoroughly inspect the structure to identify any structural problems. This will entail removing doors and drawers, and all hardware.

The best cabinets are made of dovetailed joints, and those are likely to still be in good shape. Box or butt joints are more common but less secure and chances are, if the cabinet is fairly old, you'll need to reinforce the joints to one degree or another. You may also need to square up the cabinet so that it doesn't sag or hang out of true.

BRACING CORNERS

There are many different options for reinforcing wobbly cabinet joints, and you can use a combination of them if necessary. Corner braces, also known as glue blocks, are effective solutions for a cabinet that is out of square, and once in place they reinforce the entire cabinet box structure. They are also simple to make and simple to install. Cut a 2"-square piece of 1" nominal board (hardwood is preferable) and saw the square in half diagonally. Use bar clamps to square up the cabinet,

checking the corners for square with a carpenter's square. Coat the edges of the block with wood glue and position it in the corner of the cabinet, on level with the top edge of the cabinet. Brace all four corners of the cabinet, and allow the glue to dry completely before removing the bar clamps. Where the cabinet structure is very tenuous, you can drill pilot holes through the blocks and nail them into place for additional strength. A quicker and easier solution for functional utility cabinets is to brace the corners with steel angle braces. Screw the braces into place with 1/2″ screws. Steel corner plates are a way to secure the corners without marring the interior look of the cabinet. To install corner plates, use a chisel to create a mortise in the corner down into which the corner plate will be screwed.

RECONSTITUTING JOINTS

Some well-made cabinets will be joined with dovetail joints that can withstand gravity and the ravages of time virtually unscathed. But more commonly, cabinets are joined with box joints or simple butt joints. These can separate as adhesive degrades and fasteners loosen over time. If a joint in the face frame or carcass of a cabinet has separated slightly, you can restore it by using a glue syringe to inject wood glue into the joint, and then clamping the joint until the adhesive dries. This method can also be used to renew the joints in a cabinet drawer.

SALVAGE WISDOM

Nailed joints are susceptible to time, gravity, and wear and tear, just as glued joints are. If you are reviving a reclaimed cabinet and find that nails are missing or are too loose in their holes, the best idea is to replace them with screws. Drill countersunk holes for the screws over the nail holes, and plug the holes after you've installed the screws. Where screws have stripped in their holes, you can glue a dowel into the hole and then screw into the dowel.

Chapter 3

—✸—

SALVAGING
OLD METAL

The uses for the various metals pulled out of aged buildings and newer renovations are not quite as obvious or wide-ranging as they are with reclaimed wood. But that's not to say that there aren't plenty of home-design applications for reclaimed metal fixtures and building materials. Tin panels that covered the ceilings of the yesterday can be repurposed to clad just about any surface in a new home. Reclaimed plumbing pipe can be pressed into service as bookshelf brackets or for the frame of a hanging pot rack. You just have to be a little more creative in exploiting the potential of reclaimed metal than you would be in re-using a wood floor, for instance.

There are really two basic types of metal reclaimed in the process of deconstruction: metal fixtures such as metal cabinets, iron radiators, and vintage tin ceilings are most often used in their original states, in applications similar to those from which they were removed. Metal structures, such as copper and iron pipes, flashing, and tin siding are usually adapted to a new and innovative use. Most of the metal salvaged from buildings falls into the latter category.

In the normal course of business, demolition companies and contractors doing demolition work would sell most of the metal recovered from a building to a scrap dealer. The scrap dealer would recycle the material, or pass it along to a third party—such as a smelting operation—for recycling. Traditionally, this has been one of the "green" parts of building demolition and renovation.

However, reclaiming and reusing these materials is even greener. When you repurpose metal grates, radiators, steel doors and other similar leftovers, you are saving the energy it would take to melt them down for recycling. You're also saving the waste products inherent in the metal recycling process. That's one of the things that make reusing reclaimed materials in home design so attractive. The other, of course, is the actual appearance of what you create.

Reclaimed metal materials that are inherently attractive are the easiest to adapt into a home's design. For instance, finding a new purpose for tin ceilings is not a huge challenge to the imagination. They can be used to embellish just about any flat surface, from a divider wall, to a backsplash, to a tabletop, and even a new ceiling. The point is, the form of the material carries with it a certain cachet of beauty that makes reuse fairly easy. The same is true of cast iron grillwork used over heating vents, as window security, and in other forms. Even radiators are easily pressed into service as eye-catching table bases because their forms are simply striking.

On the other hand, if you're willing to stretch your creative muscles a little, you'll find plenty of uses for more mundane salvaged metals. Plumbing pipe, whether it's copper, cast iron, black iron, or galvanized steel, can be reused in a number of innovative ways. And working with these plumbing fundamentals is easy because the skills you'll need are a snap to master, and the tools for working with pipe are probably already in your toolbox. Even if they aren't, they are relatively inexpensive additions.

Whether you've picked out some rare copper tiles to grace a breakfast bar skirting, or have decided to create a set of book shelves from a jumble of galvanized iron pipes, you'll soon discover another wonderful thing about repurposing metal building materials: they are relatively inexpensive. Because bringing these types of materials back to life involves both imagination and elbow grease, building owners and salvage firms alike are usually willing to part with them for a song.

Pressed sheet metal can be used for decorative projects, either as-is or in revived form.

A little prep work and painting is all that's needed to make these radiators eye-catching bases for a low table.

TYPES OF RECLAIMED METALS

TIN

The most engaging form of tin is the pressed tin ceiling panels common to early 20th century buildings. These are very desirable because the designs are often unique and fascinating, and there are a vast variety of different patterns. The panels, usually 24 inches square, can be reused in a number of different ways. They can also be painted, distressed, or left natural, increasing the potential surface appearances. Couple the desirable look with the fact that many tin ceilings are destroyed in removal, and it's no wonder that these are also some of the more expensive metal remnants you're going to find in a salvage company's stock. However, you can realize a bargain if you manage to get in at the source and reclaim a tin ceiling yourself. They are not terribly difficult to remove, but require caution to prevent damaging the panels. Galvanized corrugated tin sheets or seamed panels are another type that is often removed from older buildings (especially outbuildings with tin sheet roofs), and structures such as water towers. The sheets can be repuposed as ceilings or walls—either inside or outside—for a handsome, rugged contrast to more sedate sheetrock surfaces.

COPPER

One of the most purely beautiful metals, copper is usually salvaged in the form of pipes. The pipes can be cut, cleaned, and reconnected to make interesting and useful structures like the pot rack described on page 86. Or, you may have enough leftover pipe from a plumbing project that you can take on a small building project with this versatile material. Much more rarely, you'll find vintage hammered copper tiles used for walls or counters. Because you're not likely to find a large quantity of these, they are best used as decorative accent pieces—either in a tiled pattern or as stand alone decorations. Regardless of the form it takes, any copper needs to be sealed to retain its shiny red appearance. However, unsealed copper will eventually oxidize, resulting in a sophisticated light green matte patina that many people prefer.

IRON

Iron is one of the most abundant building materials reclaimed from older buildings. There are two basic forms of iron used in buildings: cast and wrought. Cast iron is poured into molds and used to make objects that require precise dimensions or are copied for mass reproduction, such as pipes, vent covers, and window grills. Wrought iron is handworked into forms usually unique to the building and any wrought-iron piece is usually interesting in and of itself. That said, many cast-iron architectural elements are made in beautiful forms that can be used as is. Cast iron is also incredibly strong, so cast-iron pieces are often used in design projects that require structural reinforcement.

RECLAIMED TIN CEILINGS

Beautifully ornate tin ceilings first saw widespread use in the late 1800s, and their use continues to the present day. However, whereas they are now used for purely decorative purposes, they originally had both a decorative and a functional purpose. They were handsome alternatives to, and imitations of, the decorative ceiling plasterwork common in homes of the wealthy. But they were also fireproof surfaces in kitchens with dicey wiring and where open flames were still the order of the day. But whatever their practical applications, the popularity of tin ceilings grew and grew, largely due to the unique appearance of the surface.

Tin ceilings were crafted in an astounding range of relief designs, with period styles from the baroque, to Victorian, to Arts & Crafts and Art Deco, and many more. Literally dozens of styles were created. Although manufacturers of modern reproductions do an admirable job of re-creating the most popular designs, you are still likely to chance upon a completely unique look in a home being deconstructed, or at your local salvage materials vendor. It's just the nature of the industry that some design styles were lost in the pages of history. Add to that the fact that the designs of field tiles (the general tiles used across the ceiling) are complimented by visually unique centerpiece medallions, filler tiles featuring plainer patterns, cornice pieces that bridged the seams between ceiling and wall, and specialized molding pieces that embellished the look even more. All of which means that with a little effort and a bit of luck, you can have a one-of-kind look for many different surfaces in your home.

That's because although you can certainly re-use a tin ceiling exactly as it was initially intended—as a ceiling covering—you can also use it on just about any other flat surface. Tin ceilings make remarkable wall coverings, and are often repurposed as wainscoting and to decorate an accent wall, or an entire country kitchen. The tin panels can be cut down and repurposed as kitchen cabinet inserts, or used in a more modern kitchen as an intricate and interesting backsplash. Some people even use the material as a unique covering for a table top.

Before you use tin ceiling panels, you need to reclaim them. That can be a messy job if you're salvaging a ceiling from an existing building. But even if you are buying panels from a salvage company, it's likely that they have not stripped and refinished the tin. Most tin rescued from older buildings will not only be covered in degraded paint, it will also likely carry a coating of grime from airborne pollutants such as the grease residue from cooking. At a bare minimum, the tin will require a good cleaning prior to re-use. More likely, it will need to be stripped down to bare metal and refinished with paint or a sealant such as polyurethane.

In cleaning and stripping pieces of a tin ceiling, you may be surprised to find a different surface than tin. Tin ceiling panels were actually tin-plated steel, to create a more structurally sound surface that was less prone to flexing. Less often, though, the panels were plated in copper or bronze. Both of these provide a highly desirable look, and they are usually covered in a clear finish and placed in a highly visible location to show off the beautiful metal.

Either way, once you've cleaned up the panels, working with them is easy. Armed with tin snips, pliers, and a good set of thick gloves, you'll be ready to bring glory to whatever surface you're decorating.

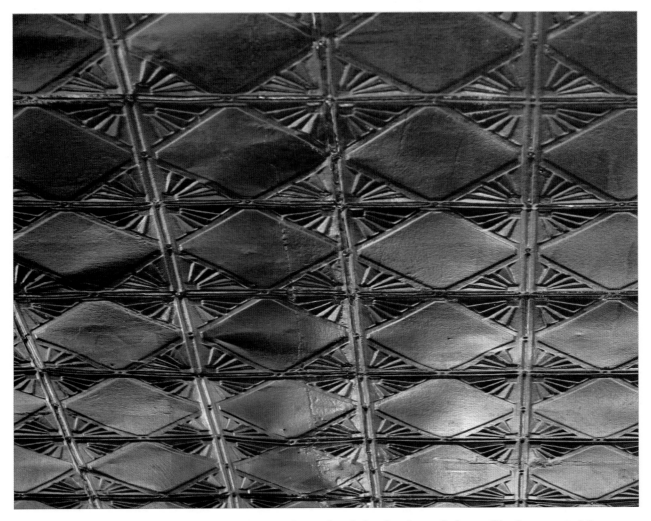

Reclaimed tin ceiling panels look best if you can retain some of the antique feel—otherwise, you're better off buying new material.

RECLAIMING A TIN CEILING

Tin ceiling panels are some of the easiest metal materials to reclaim from an existing structure. Although the work is dirty, it's not a challenge to your DIY skills and it's not even all that physically demanding. Given the cost of reproduction tin panels, the few hours you'll spend taking down and reclaiming an existing ceiling will be time well spent.

Tin ceilings were originally mounted on a grid of wood lath; if you're reclaiming a ceiling in an older home, that's probably what you'll be dealing with. Fancier versions may also have cornice running around the seam between ceilings and walls, and may even feature "flat molding," special profile pieces that separate a center square of more decorative field panels from an outer border of plainer filler panels. All of these pieces can be reclaimed and repurposed.

To take down the ceiling, start with the outermost pieces first, working your way toward the center. If there is a cornice, start with the corner cornice piece that isn't overlapped by any other. Pry it (this shouldn't take much effort because time and structural movement will have loosened the nails' grip) away from the wall, using a small pry bar with a thin, flat prying edge. Continue stripping pieces of the cornice,

jimmying it at nail locations along the panels. Stack them on top of each other in short piles.

Next, you'll begin working on the filler panels if there are any, and the field panels if there aren't. Pry each panel down from the outside, taking care not to excessively bend the panel. As you pry, it will help if you pull the panel toward you. Once one or two edges are loosened, the panels should come down fairly easily. Any stubborn panels should come down with careful prying and pulling.

Watch for any unexpected debris as you take panels down off the ceiling. A lot of debris, dust, and insulation may come out as you remove panels. Work slowly and you're less likely to take a dirt shower.

Stack the panels in short piles and make separate piles for field and filler tiles. It's a good idea to secure each pile for transportation by binding it with twine or duct tape, after sandwiching the pile between top and bottom pieces of cardboard. Store the panels indoors, in a garage or shed, where they won't be exposed to moisture. Although it's likely that the face of the panels will be covered in paint, the backsides will probably be unfinished and susceptible to rust.

Metal ceiling panels can be inset into a recessed area, such as this coffered porch ceiling, to turn them into a focal point.

✚ SAFETY FIRST

Taking down a tin ceiling is not terribly hard work because gravity is on your side. But the force that brings the ceiling down can also bring down decades of accumulated debris. There are really two main safety hazards when deconstructing the ceiling: sharp edges and airborne material. Because tin ceilings predated the widespread use of asbestos as an insulating material, it's not a common concern when tearing out an original tin ceiling in a very old home. However, other material, including compacted dirt from the floors or attic above, and mold can create a lung-harming cloud. Always wear extremely tough work gloves and a thick, long-sleeve work shirt or jacket to avoid serious cuts from the edges of the tin panels. Wear a hat, respirator, and wraparound eye protection to ensure that the work doesn't take an unexpected toll on you.

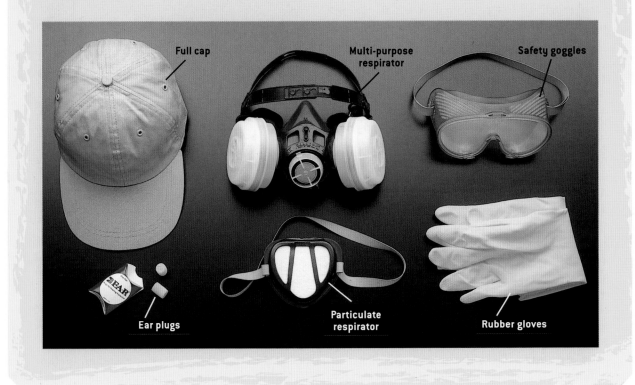

Full cap · Multi-purpose respirator · Safety goggles · Ear plugs · Particulate respirator · Rubber gloves

CLEANING & PREPPING TIN PANELS

Chances are that any tin ceiling panels you reclaim will need a good cleaning before they can be reused. In some cases, you'll be using the panels just as they are for the charm of a vintage appearance. In other situations, you may want to completely remove the old finish so that you can either display a copper or bronze surface to its best advantage, or repaint a tin panel.

There are two types of chemical strippers, those with methylene chloride and those without it. Non-methylene chloride strippers are much less toxic and can be used inside with modest ventilation. Methylene chloride strippers, however, are very toxic and should not be used inside without appropriately rated ventilation.

Either way, the process of getting a tin panel clean is sequential—start with the mildest option, and work to the most caustic.

The first step, and the one all reclaimed tin panels, cornice, and molding should go through, is a basic washing. This will not only remove obvious dirt, but it will allow you to assess the integrity of the finish underneath that dirt. You may be surprised at how easily a little soap and water can bring a painted tin panel back to life. Use a mixture of lukewarm water and mild dish soap in a sprayer. Spray the panel and scrub lightly with a stiff nylon scrub brush. The dish soap will usually remove even stubborn layers of grease. Dry the panel immediately after you've washed it, using a clean, dry towel. Never leave a tin panel to air dry because that is just inviting rust.

A good cleaning will often reveal a still attractive finish on a tin panel. But if you find loose or flaking paint, or simply hope to repaint the panel, you'll need to get down to a stable, rough surface to which the primer and topcoat can adhere. Use a drill equipped with a wire wheel to remove any loose paint, apparent dirt, and rough up the paint that is left. If you are planning on finishing the surface natural with a clear coat of polyurethane, you should strip the paint using a chemical stripper or—the more environmentally friendly option—soak the panel in a hot water-and-soap bath. You'll need a large tub, but this solution can be incredibly effective for stripping paint off tin panels. You can polish the surface of a tin ceiling panel or border piece using a buffing wheel and polish specially formulated for whichever metal surface covers the panel.

A heat gun is usually the quickest way to strip multiple layers of paint. Apply the heat evenly across the surface just until the paint bubbles or rises up. Then scrape off the paint with a plastic paint scraper, using a stiff nylon brush if you're going to ultimately finish the surface natural, or a wire brush if you'll be painting the surface, to remove paint stuck in the recesses of ornate embossing. For stubborn paint caught in the small crevices of ornate tin panel designs, you may need to finish with chemical paint stripper.

Paint strippers are the last resort when it comes to cleaning up a tin panel. You should be careful in selecting a stripper that will not react to the tin plating or the metal underneath (you'll find strippers that are

A wire wheel attachment can be highly effective in removing surface debris from the nooks and crannies of a tin panel's design. But it should only be used on a tin panel that will be repainted, not finished natural.

specially formulated for use on metals at your local home center). Brush the stripper across the surface, being generous with the application. Follow the manufacturer's instructions, which usually require that the stripper be allowed to sit on the surface for several hours. Scrape off the paint and repeat if necessary.

➕ SAFETY FIRST

The edges of cut tin panels can be extremely sharp. That not only presents a potential hazard for your arms and hands, it can be an even bigger danger for electrical fixtures and wiring. When installing make sure that any cuts around an electrical box opening do not leave sharp edges in the way of wiring or the fixture body. The edges should be rolled if possible, or hammered flat if not. No edges or metal should protrude into the actual electrical box or sit against a light fixture body.

INSTALL A TIN BACKSPLASH

The space between countertop and cabinet bottom is often a wasted home design opportunity. Because you don't actually use the surface, it's all too easy to overlook the design potential of a backsplash. But this particular area is ideal for cladding in reclaimed tin. It's a modest enough surface that the tin won't overwhelm the kitchen, but the exposure is visible enough that you'll get a lot of bang for the buck from this particular design accent.

The techniques used here are incredibly simple, and the materials and tools needed are all quite basic as well. You should be able to put up a tin backsplash in the space of an afternoon without breaking a sweat. What's more, this same process can be used to put up tin wainscoting, clad a pantry door, or even cover an accent wall in reclaimed tin panels. We've used construction adhesive to hold up the panels here, which should be fine for your kitchen as well, however, if you want to take extra precautions, you can nail the panels to studs, nailing through the nailing rails on the panels. One caveat though—in dealing with cut tin, you'll be working with very sharp edges. A moment of inattention can result in a fairly serious cut. Always use the thickest work gloves you can find, and be careful when manipulating panels into position.

You'll also want to seal both the surface and seams of the backsplash. The kitchen is home to many spills and splashes, and any moisture that makes it underneath the backsplash panels can lead to rust and, potentially, mold. That's why you'll seal all the edges with clear caulk, and seal the surface in a clear finish or high-gloss paint.

These reclaimed metal ceiling panels make a beautiful and comment-generating kitchen sink backsplash.

(Continued)

1 Measure the backsplash area, including the location of any wall switches or outlets. Look at the embossed design on the tin panels and determine where you want them positioned, and what overall pattern you want to create along the length of the backsplash.

2 Lay the tin panels out on a clean, flat work surface to determine their final positioning. Mark the layout lines on the face of the tin panels for cutting, using a black marker and a metal straightedge. Mark the position of all wall switches or outlet cutouts. Cut the first panel to fit.

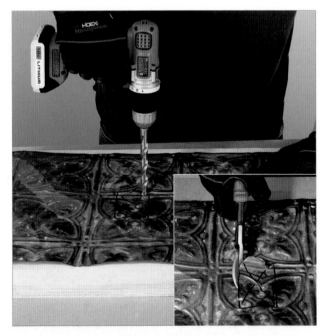

3 Make the cutouts for switches or outlets by drilling a large hole at one corner of the area to be cut out. Use tin snips (inset) to widen the hole, and then cut along the cutout line and remove the cutout.

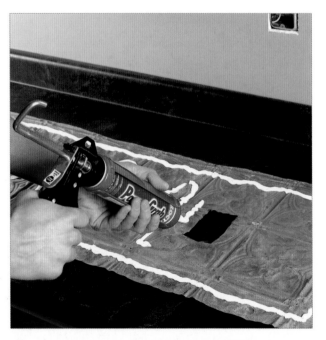

4 Coat the back of the first panel with construction adhesive in a serpentine pattern. The pattern should distribute adhesive evenly over the surface. But keep adhesive away from the panel's edges to avoid any squeeze-out during installation.

5 Position the panel in place on the wall, and press it down. Make sure the entire surface is firmly in contact with the backsplash surface.

6 Coat the back of the next panel with construction adhesive and place it into position. The panels should overlap at the edge nailing rails. Be careful not to spread adhesive onto adjacent panels.

7 Secure the panels in place by taping them together with painter's tape or duct tape. You should leave the tape in place until you're absolutely sure the construction adhesive has fully set and the panels are stable.

8 Caulk around the edges of the panels using tinted (available from aftermarket tin ceiling manufacturers) or clear caulk, in the seam between the tin and the countertops, and between the tops of the panels and the bottoms of the cabinets. Lay a bead of caulk along the edges in corners as necessary to ensure a watertight seal for the backsplash.

SALVAGED PLUMBING PIPE

Plumbing pipe, although plentiful in deconstruction and demolition projects, is more of a challenge to reuse than wood or other metals. Plumbing pipe does not have the original and apparent decorative application that something like a wood floor or tin ceiling would. In that sense, it's not obviously attractive—it requires adaptation. In addition, contractors and deconstruction firms alike tend to recycle pipe rather than try to sell it for reuse. There are many recycling operations dealing in scrap metal, so if you're going to reclaim pipe, you need to get in at the source, or find the rare reseller who stocks pipe.

But that effort can pay off in spades. When and where you do find it, reclaimed plumbing pipe of all sorts is generally very inexpensive. Pipe is also easy to work with, strong, and durable. Most pipe is fairly innocuous in appearance. Copper pipe is the exception. Like other copper fixtures, the finish on copper pipe and tubing can be alluring. But even if you are faced with using another type of pipe, you can change the look to suit your needs and tastes. Plumbing pipes can be sanded and polished smooth, left natural, or painted any color of the rainbow.

Whatever type you choose, stay away from lead pipe and pipes that were used to carry solid waste. Even though you're not likely to use lead pipe in a project near food, there's too great a chance that the pipe can degrade and flake, creating a potentially toxic situation inside the home. Likewise, sewage pipes carry the risk of contamination.

Use plumbing pipe in a design project and you'll inevitably need to use companion fittings. These include elbows that allow you to turn corners, T fittings that enable supporting connections, reducers, and mounting flanges, among others. These fittings allow you to combine piping into various structures, and also aid in mounting a finished project to a wall, floor, or ceiling.

TYPES OF RECLAIMED PLUMBING PIPE

COPPER

This is by far the most attractive type of plumbing pipe. Unless they've become corroded for some reason, the finish should be shiny and deep red, creating a look that complements a wide range of decors. The metal is also very easy to work with and can even be bent fairly simply. Joints are usually soldered because it is difficult to tap threads onto the end of a thin copper wall. Copper pipes used in home design are usually sealed against corrosion, although they can be left unfinished or even lightly sanded to speed up the aging process that results in a fetching green patina. The patina itself will itself ultimately protect the surface.

IRON

The two basic types of iron pipes widely used in homes and other structures are cast iron and black iron. For the purposes of reuse in design projects, the differences are minimal. Although black iron is a bit softer and generally used for gas lines, any type of iron pipe is very strong, and certainly strong enough for just about any design re-use project you might have in mind. Although strong, cast iron is brittle, which makes cutting or reshaping the material a bit of a challenge. Smaller diameter pipes can be cut with a hacksaw, while large pipes are better severed with a snap cutter, available from most rental stores. Both black- and cast-iron pipes can be sanded down, primed, and painted. Without the changing temperature of water or gas running through them, the pipes' surface will remain stable for a long time.

GALVANIZED STEEL PIPE

For the purposes of a design project, galvanized pipe is not so very different from iron pipe. The two could not be more distinct when it comes to plumbing. The pipe is formed by dipping a steel tube into a bath of zinc, chemically bonding the two metals and giving the pipe its signature dull gray-silver appearance. Because galvanized plumbing pipe predates copper pipe in general use, much of the plumbing pipe you're likely to find on demolition or deconstruction projects will be galvanized. The pipe can be cut with a pipe cutter, but is otherwise threaded and worked much like iron pipe is. It is also strong enough for most home design applications.

DESOLDERING COPPER PIPE

1 Carefully heat the joint. Move the torch around the joint quickly without stopping. Keep the flame an inch or so from the surface of the metal. Attempt to heat the joint evenly.

2 As the solder heats, liquefies, and begins to flow out of the joint, suck it up with a vacuum pump (known commonly as a "solder sucker"). As the flow decreases, you can capture the last of the solder with a soldering wick.

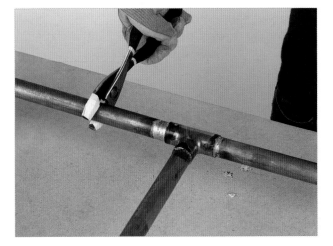

3 Gently and firmly pull the joint or pipes apart using large pliers with rubber grips and jaws that you've padded with masking tape or other protective covering to ensure against marking the metal. If the pieces don't come apart easily, reheat the joint until they do.

CONSTRUCT A COPPER PIPE POT RACK

No cook's kitchen is complete without a pot rack. It's a way to store interesting items in plain view, and it makes pots and pans much more accessible. You can buy pot racks in just about any style under the sun, but why pay for something that is so easy to make yourself?

The rack described here measures 3 feet long by 2 feet wide, which is a useful size for most small to medium kitchens. However, one of the wonderful things about working with reclaimed pipe—especially soft pipe such as the copper plumbing pipe used in this project—is how easy it is to cut to size. You can customize this project to any size that suits you, but keep the cross braces, which are important for maintaining the rack's shape, under the weight of various pots and pans.

Another wonderful thing about this pot rack—and about working with reclaimed plumbing pipe in general—is that it doesn't require a lot of expertise or specialized tools. The copper pipe we've used here is especially accommodating for the DIYer with basic skills. The pipe does not need to be tapped with new threads when you cut it because it is simply soldered into the connectors and adaptors used to construct the rack.

But the best reason for choosing copper pipe is the sheer beauty of the material. Not only is it attractive in its own right, copper just seems to fit right into a kitchen. We've mounted this eye-catching rack on solid supports, also made of copper pipe, screwed into ceiling joists. However, some homeowners prefer a pot rack with a little swing to it. If that's the case, mount the rack by screwing substantial eye bolts into ceiling joists, and hanging the rack by chains and S hooks. You can buy the hardware in copper or other metals at most home centers or hardware stores.

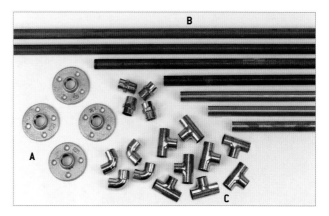

The parts for this project include: mounting flanges (A); leftover copper tubing (B); and copper pipe fittings (C).

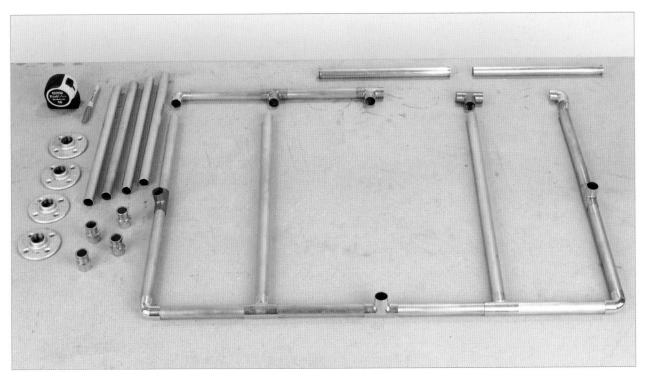

1 Lay out the pieces you'll use for the rack on a flat, level work surface. Mark pieces for cutting as necessary to match the dimensions of the rack. Remember to account for the portion of the tube or pipe that will go inside fittings such as elbows. Be sure to factor in the support posts and mounting flanges if you are hanging the rack from fixed posts.

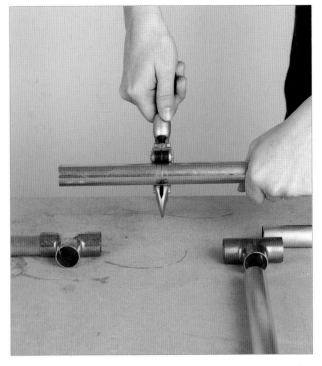

2 Cut sections of the pipe as necessary using a tubing cutter. Set the pipe in the cutter so that the cutting wheel is aligned with the marked cut line. Screw the clamp down to tighten the wheel on the pipe and begin rotating the cutter around the pipe.

3 Burnish the ends of cut pipes and insides of connecters using 000 steel wool or a burnishing tool. After you're done, the end of the pipe should be clean and shiny. Burnish the insides of the fitting into which the pipe will be soldered.

(Continued)

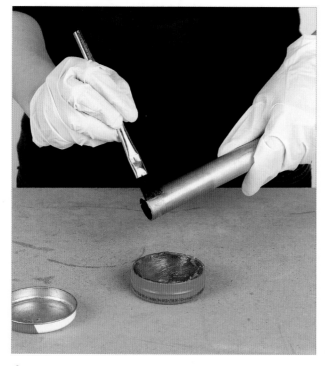

4 Apply flux around the end of a pipe to be soldered. The surface should be absolutely clean before you start. Use the flux brush to spread flux liberally around the end of the pipe.

✚ SAFETY FIRST

Most solder contains lead. So, whether you are desoldering to disassemble copper pipe that you've reclaimed from an old structure, or are soldering to construct a project such as the one shown here, effective ventilation is essential. If you are working in a workshop, garage, or other indoor space, use a strong fan positioned directly over your work surface, and vented to an outside window. If you'll be doing a lot of soldering or desoldering, consider using a respirator rated for lead fumes or lead-free solder.

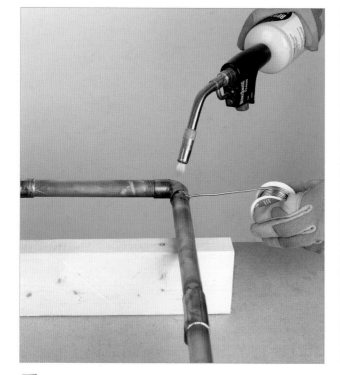

5 Touch the solder to the pipe. It should melt on contact. Apply the solder in a bead around the joint. Touch up the soldered joint as necessary, but do not touch the pipe until it has fully cooled down from the soldering process. Once the pipe has cooled, burnish the joint with 000 steel wool.

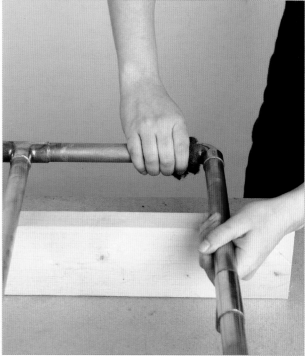

6 Slip the pipe into the fitting, making sure that they are fully engaged. Light the torch and begin sweating the joint. Move the flame along the joint, back and forth, until it is completely heated—about 30 seconds.

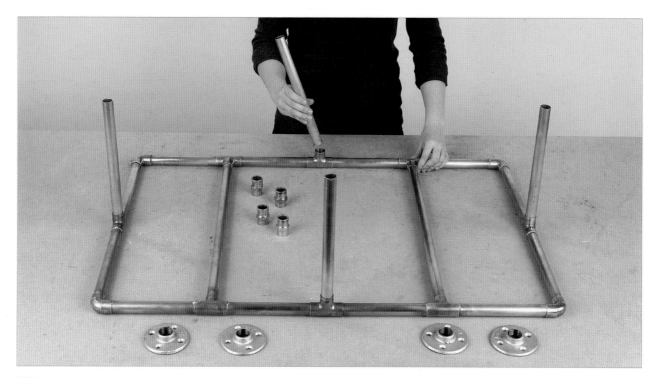

7 Continue soldering pieces together, soldering the inner braces first, and then completing the outer frame. Be sure that fittings for fixed hanging posts are positioned perfectly perpendicular to the frame. Check on a level surface that the rack lays flat. If it doesn't you'll need to heat up the problem joints and re-solder them.

8 With the rack frame complete, solder the hanging posts into place in the T fittings on the frame. Screw copper male threaded adapters into the mounting flanges. Drill 1/8" pilot holes through each adapter, slide it onto the pole, and screw in a 1/2" self-tapping metal screw.

9 Hold the rack up in the mounting location and mark the flange screw holes on the ceiling along ceiling joists. Drill pilot holes and hang the rack by screwing three #10 wood screws through the flange and into the ceiling joists.

Chapter 4

—⁓—

RECLAIMING STONE MATERIALS

Stone endures. Even as a building ages and crumbles, the stone components remain unscathed. That's why the many types of natural stone—and their kiln-fired cousins—are prime candidates for salvaging and reuse. The forms stone and ceramics take are many and varied and, in most cases, incredibly beautiful. They can be reused as decoration, structural elements, or, more commonly, as both. Some, such as carved marble fireplace mantels, are best used as they were originally intended. Others, such as foundation stones or cobblestones, can be reused in many different and even surprising ways. The versatile nature of the material and beguiling range of appearances make stone and ceramics popular reclaimed materials. No matter what your individual home design project may entail, reclaimed stone or ceramic of some sort can play a compelling role.

Stone and its manmade equivalents have been used as building materials for thousands of years. Ancient Romans used decorative stone tile throughout their sumptuous homes. The English built many of their most iconic and lasting structures of locally quarried stone. Closer to home, early pioneers in this country built solid, lasting structures with foundations or entire walls constructed of fieldstone. The trend continues to the modern day, with the best buildings including some elements of stone and ceramics.

Such a rich history teaches us that stone is an incredibly useful building material. It can also be incredibly enchanting. As much as builders have been drawn to the inherent strength in stone and ceramics, homeowners, designers, and others have been captivated by the inherent beauty of stone surfaces. There seems to be an endless variety to capture the eye: flecks and veining, colors in every shade, and intriguing surface textures.

There are almost as many ways to use the material as there are variations in appearances. Anywhere you might want or need a durable, engaging surface, some type of stone, brick, or other ceramic creation will serve admirably.

USES FOR RECLAIMED STONE & CERAMICS

COUNTERTOPS AND BACKSPLASHES

Stone surfaces and reclaimed tile often come from salvaged countertops, so it makes sense that they would be reused in that role. But even if the materials are rescued from somewhere else in a deconstructed home, they are still prime candidates to serve as countertops. Floor tiles, such as large format (12" x 12") or larger can easily be resuscitated as countertops even if the tiles need to be cut to fit. Terra cotta tiles salvaged from a floor or a patio, and ceramic tiles of all sorts, can be repurposed into counters or backsplashes. Just be clear that you will likely have to do some modifications and special fitting because many older tiles are not standardized sizes. Stone slabs can provide even more dramatic countertop options. However, you may need to cut slabs to fit—a possibly daunting job if the slab is unusually thick. Stone slabs may also need to be sealed or otherwise finished before they can be used as countertops in the kitchen or bathroom.

MANTELS

Whether it's a mantel over the fireplace or a decorative mantel along an entry wall, no mantel is more impressive than one made of stone. You can choose from a more precise and formal look of cut stone, such as a granite curbstone, or more visually intriguing raw stone. A stone mantel can be a room's showpiece, but it is also a challenge to mount because of the weight and the fact that the back surface of the mantel has to be completely flat. But with the proper installation and appropriate reinforcement, a stone mantel will last the life of the building.

FIREPLACE SURROUNDS

Stone has long been the material of choice for cladding indoor fireplaces in a beautiful, fireproof, and virtually

indestructible material that is also relatively inexpensive. These structures come in two different forms—carved stone surrounds reclaimed as a single piece, often including hearth, surround, and mantel, and loose stones that are stacked in place—mortared or not—to create a unique and handsome structure. Carved surrounds are generally hard to find, coming from larger, more opulent houses. They can be incredibly impressive and can visually dominate a room, but all that design power comes with a hefty price tag. You'll pay for both the stone itself and the craftsmanship of the carving. Loose stones, such as ledgestone or stacked flagstone, create a much more rustic and informal look. You'll find a far greater selection of loose stones with which to craft a fireplace surround than you will completed carved surrounds in good shape. But the most plentiful option by far will be reclaimed brick, which is also one of the easiest and most natural materials to form into a surround. And antique brick features so many surprising color variations that you may choose it over other candidates.

HORIZONTAL SURFACES

Stone slabs and stone and ceramic tiles are some of the most sumptuous and wonderful floors you can install. They are best suited to kitchens, but in some cases, a particular stone or kiln-fired material will be perfect for an entryway or even a living room. Reclaimed stone tiles and ceramic tiles often come from newer buildings that have been demolished for one reason or another. Brick and loose stone floors were common in many late 19th and early 20th-century homes, especially in the South. Stone, terra cotta tile, or brick floors can be reclaimed in their entirety when you find them, and the aging may have added a wonderfully worn surface. The looks you can achieve range from farmhouse to Mediterranean, rural to sophisticated, and beyond. Whenever you're considering a reclaimed stone floor—especially if it's replacing wood or carpet—keep in mind that the surface will be colder underfoot year round.

PATHWAYS

Just as they make wonderful floors within a house, stones of all kinds make excellent pavers for an unforgettable patio, garden path, a walkway, or even a driveway. Outdoor surfaces are a natural use of any stone or kiln-fired material, because there is an organic connection between the material and outdoor area. Any flat stone can be used in this way: slate, granite sidewalk slabs, and unfinished marble countertop pieces to name just a few. Of course, dimensional pavers such as bricks and cobblestones are also perfect for these types of surfaces. The basic choice you're ultimately going to

make is whether you want an irregular design, such as you'd get with a flagstone patio, or the more regimented look you'd get in laying a surface such as a herringbone brick pathway.

TYPES OF RECLAIMED STONE

GRANITE

Justly famous as being one of the hardest and most durable stone surfaces, granite is also one of the more elegant. The colors are all dusty muted shades, most typically light and dark gray. But, although they're rare, you can also find more vibrant shades of granite, including light reds, black, and purples. If you're lucky enough to reclaim a granite countertop, it's best used as a countertop. But other forms have several different uses. Most of the granite you'll encounter on job sites or at salvage yards will be unfinished, unpolished, and unsealed. The surface will be a dusty matte, but the interesting surface graining still creates exceptional visual appeal. Granite is most often reclaimed in the form of curbstones—mantel-shaped pieces that served as barriers between early sidewalks and streets—cobblestones, and some flagstones that are mostly reclaimed from overseas sources. Curbs and cobblestones are often worn down a bit, and for that reason make wonderful choices for flooring inside and out. Curbstones are regularly used as steps to accent a stone floor, or outside as a surface impervious to the elements. They also make wonderful mantels and fireplace hearths. If you use reclaimed granite on the inside of the house, you should be aware that although the stone is hard, it is also porous—it absorbs liquids and will stain if you spill something like wine on the surface. For a high gloss look, you'll need to polish the surface; for a water- and stain-resistant surface, you'll need to seal it.

LIMESTONE

This common building stone was used in early settler barns, walls, fences, and outbuildings, because it was often easier to find and stack the stone than it was to cut down and mill lumber. It was also widely used in commercial buildings around the turn of the 20th century for its handsome chalky white appearance, with relatively large open pores (some pinkish, orange, and off-white colorations appear less frequently). The stone's appearance is due to the fact that it is a sedimentary rock formed by the deposit of fossils, decaying marine life, sand, and other calcium-based sediments. You can choose between domestic and imported limestone available through suppliers, or you may be lucky enough to deconstruct a very old barn or pump house made of the stacked stone. Regardless, limestone can be used for countertops, a warm-climate floor, or even a patio surface, although indoors the stone should be sealed. Lesser grades are frequently stacked as the stone originally was to make a neat fireplace surround. Limestone can also be used for garden walls or low borders. Travertine is a version of limestone with a sophisticated, slightly mottled surface appearance similar to marble. Travertine comes in rich amber yellows, whites, dusty reds, and black.

SANDSTONE

Another sedimentary stone, sandstone was formed on the banks of rivers, made of sand and silt (thus the name). You are unlikely to reclaim sandstone, because much of the reclaimed stone is imported from Europe where it has historically been used in buildings. Because of the way it was formed, pieces of sandstone can have intriguing flowing variations, such as a darker brown streak across a regular light brown surface. Generally though, the surface pattern is regular and tightly grained, in tan or caramel. Some sandstone is, however, black, and others can range from pink to terra cotta red. The color depends on what other materials, such as iron, were present when the stone was formed. Sandstone can be used in the same applications as limestone—countertops, flooring, and wall tiles. But where moisture is present, the stone needs to be sealed. It can also be finished in any sheen, from pure matte to high gloss. No matter where you use it, or how you finish it, you'll find that sandstone is durable and long-wearing, and ages well.

FIELDSTONE AND FLAGSTONE

Settlers on the plains quickly discovered that there were a great deal of usable stones in the ground all around them. Called fieldstones and flagstones because they were harvested from fields, these stones were used to build houses, barns, walls, and other structures. Fieldstones are round and boulder-like. Flagstones are flat and break apart in layers. The stones are commonly reclaimed in abundant amounts. Fieldstone is a bit more difficult to work with and is usually mortared into place. Flagstone is often stacked dry to create everything from low garden walls to fireplace surrounds to skirting for a breakfast bar. Fieldstone and flagstone blend well with any natural surrounding, making ideal patio or pathway surfaces, although the stones are rarely used for flooring or countertops inside the house. Both of these have a coarse earthy surface and earth tone colorings, and are best used in an informal country lodge or other rustic décors.

SLATE

This extremely hard and durable stone is reclaimed from antique floors, roof tiles, and interior applications such as fireplace hearths. Because of the many areas both inside and out from which slate is recovered, you can find standardized cut tiles, and larger, irregular slabs that can be reused in a number of different ways. Slate is often laid as flooring because it is far less porous than other options such as granite, and the uneven surface texture makes the stone slip-resistant. These same properties

make slate a good choice for countertops, although this is a far less common application. Slate can also make an excellent wall cladding. Large slabs can be cut for use as table tops. No matter where it's used, slate provides a lovely appearance. Surface patterns vary by variety, and include interesting veining, apparent graining, or nearly solid colored surfaces. The colors range from black and deep purple to the more common grays and dusty blues to turquoise and light reds. Combinations of these colors in the same slab surface are not uncommon.

WORKING WITH STONE TILES & SLABS

Reclaimed stone tiles, countertops, and slabs can be some of the best bargains in a salvage yard. The cost of these is often a 30-percent or more reduction of the price of the same materials if purchased new. Of course, there are tradeoffs. Reclaimed tiles, countertops, and other forms may not be standardized thicknesses. Be prepared (as you always should be in working with any reclaimed materials) to deal with irregularities.

You should also be ready to do a bit of prep work to get the materials in shape for the project you have in mind. The greatest cost savings—and the biggest challenges—will come from reclaiming tiles or slab surfaces yourself. Reclaiming antique stone is a laborious process no matter what form it's in. Wall-mounted slabs such as mantels will be removed by deconstructing the wall around the stone, and then carefully prying the stone away from and off of its mounting fixtures. Reclaiming a curbstone or other stone from an outdoor location generally means prying it out of the installation. Existing countertops are removed by first removing any attachment hardware, and then carefully prying the surface free (it helps to have a helper; long surfaces should be pried away from the mounting structure at two or more points simultaneously to ensure against breakage). Reclaiming tiles depends on the method used to lay them. In most cases, you'll need to use a grout saw to remove connecting lines between tiles, and then pry them up carefully with a flat pry bar, taking your time. Resign yourself to a lot of potential breakage.

It's usually well worth the added cost to purchase stone slabs or tiles through a salvage vendor or importer. Not only do you save your labor, the stone will normally have already been prepped to one degree or another, and the selection will be much greater. In addition to traditional reclaimed materials companies, you'll find a lot of stone options at importers, because England and other parts of Europe have a rich tradition of reclaiming stone from centuries-old buildings. Much of that stone makes its way to the U.S.

No matter where you got the stone, you will probably need to cut it to the shape you need for your particular project. You will also most likely have to clean the stone. Depending on what type of stone you use, you may even need to seal the surface.

CLEANING STONE SURFACES

Most stone can be effectively cleaned with a basic mix of warm soapy water. Always use clear, unscented dish soap and lukewarm water. When cleaning reclaimed stone, first try to remove all the dirt with a soft-bristle brush or rough towel. Then test the soap-and-water mix on a discrete area. Once you're sure that the mix will not stain the surface, wash the stone thoroughly and quickly. Use a stiff scrub brush to remove any stubborn dirt or debris. Rinse thoroughly with distilled water. Immediately dry the surface as completely as you can using a soft, clean towel. Allow the stone surface to completely air dry before working with it.

Stubborn stains usually require a specialized cleaner, especially in porous stones. Different stones require different types of solutions, so the best bet is to contact a local stone worker for tips on cleaning the particular stone, or plan on positioning the surface so that the stain is hidden.

A thorough cleaning is the first step in reclaiming stone for home-design projects.

CUTTING GRANITE OR MARBLE SLABS

1 Mark the cut line on the stone surface by centering painter's or colored masking tape over the intended cut. Use a metal straightedge and utility knife to score the cut line over the tape. Remove the tape along the waste side.

2 Using an angle grinder equipped with a stone-cutting blade, cut along the line defined by the tape. The color should guide you even as the grinder kicks up dust and debris. Carefully follow the cut line to complete the cut.

CUTTING STONE WITH A WET SAW

1 Straight cuts across the surface are easily made with a wet saw. Mark the cut on the waste side with an indelible marker. Guide the stone through the saw—equipped with a stone-cutting blade—to make a clean, straight cut.

2 Make edge cutouts by scoring the three inside borders of the cutout with a chisel or carbide tip marker. Cut each edge of the cutout, and make several parallel cuts in from the outside edge to the inside edge, resetting the fence each time. Snap the pieces out of the cutout with pliers.

(Continued)

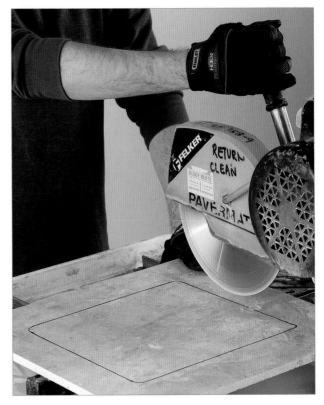

3 Clean up the cutout by positioning the tile so that the blade is sticking up inside the space of the cutout. Carefully move the tile sideways so that the blade barely skims the inside edge, cleaning up the jagged portions.

4 Make cutouts inside the field of a tile by marking the cutout and positioning the stone underneath the saw blade with the arm up. Make a plunge cut along one side of the cutout, until you almost reach the top and bottom marks. Rotate the tile and continue making plunge cuts to remove the center section.

5 Polish stone tile cut edges by equipping a grinder or power drill with a polish disc or wheel. Start polishing with an 80- to 100-grit wheel, and work sequentially down to 400 grit, until you have a perfectly smooth surface.

✚ SAFETY FIRST

Using a wet saw can be very dangerous because the saw blade is moving fast and the presence of water makes the tile very slippery to handle. Work slowly and position the fence and tile so that the part of the tile you're moving is farthest from the blade. Use safety eyewear as well, to both protect your eyes and ensure you can see as clearly as possible. When cutting with a grinder or polishing a cut stone face, use an approved dust mask and eye protection.

CUTTING SLATE

1 Thoroughly clean the slate and determine which side will be the top. Use a straightedge and marker to mark the back of the tile with the cut line. Set the tile face down on a sturdy, flat, and level surface.

2 Mark along the cut line using a sharp, pointed cold chisel, nailset, or awl. Use a hammer to tap several points about a 1/4" apart along the cut line. Use firm but light blows. The chisel only needs to mark the surface and create fracture points along the line.

3 Sandwich the marked slate tile, bottom up, between two scrap 2 x 6s. The edges of the wood should align over and under the cut line, leaving a tongue of slate hanging out on the waste side. Tap at the cut line with a maul or Stonemason's hammer.

BUILDING A GRANITE-SLAB KITCHEN ISLAND

Countertops are some of the best uses for reclaimed stone slabs. Not only are the sizes and shapes of many slabs ideal for this application, some stone surfaces were countertops in their previous incarnation. The combination of a luxurious appearance, outstanding durability, and resistance to wear and tear including physical abuse and water, make all kinds of stone ideal food preparation surfaces for the kitchen

Although we've chosen to describe adding a reclaimed stone top surface to a rolling cabinet that will serve as a mobile kitchen island, the same techniques described here can be used to adapt reclaimed stone as countertops over built-in cabinetry. Attaching the top works the same in both cases, with masonry screws holding the stone surface to the bottom structure. In both cases, as well, you may need to cut the stone you've selected to the correct size, or to make room for a sink or other feature such as a cooktop.

How you finish the stone surface is a matter both of what type of stone it is and what type of appearance you're after. Choose a slab of slate and it's possible you can seal it without polishing for a matte black or grey surface. Opt for granite, and you'll probably want to seal and finish it in a high gloss coating that is not only protective, but makes the intrinsically interesting grain really pop. Keep in mind though, that many types of stone need to be maintained if used as kitchen surfaces. Both granite and marble may need to be resealed every

six to 12 months, depending on how you've sealed them to begin with, and how they were finished.

Ultimately, though, no matter which type of reclaimed stone or finish you choose, the surface is bound to be an opulent addition to the kitchen. There is a richness to true stone—especially antique stone—that can't really be replicated in synthetic materials. Go to the effort of reclaiming a stone surface and integrating it into your kitchen's design, and you've added an unrivaled accent for a fraction of what it would cost new.

Before

100

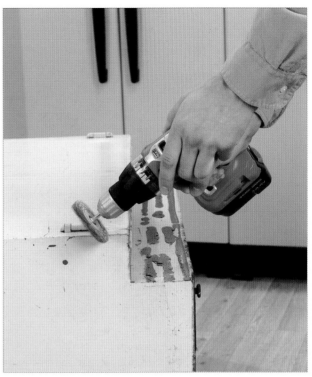

1 Remove the cabinet drawers, shelves, and all hardware for cleaning. If the hardware is in poor condition, or you find it unstylish, replace it. Check the cabinet's structure to determine if it needs reinforcement to support the stone top.

2 Prepare the cabinet for painting or finishing. Clean, sand, or just brush off rust or loose paint as necessary. Wipe down the cabinet with mineral spirits and a rag before you begin painting it.

3 Modify the cabinet as necessary. Here, metal shelf brackets are being attached to the sides to create a mounting surface for the countertop. The brackets add decorative appeal. Use decorative hex-head bolts to attach the brackets. If your cabinet has no back panel, add one.

4 Prime the cabinet carcass, doors and drawer fronts with metal primer. You'll get the best results if you use a sprayer, such as this HVLP sprayer, in a well-ventilated workroom. Make sure the primer goes on as a thin, even coat.

(Continued)

5 Paint the cabinet. For best results, apply several thin coats and use a paint formulated for metal (if your cabinet is metal). Sand lightly between coats to remove any imperfections, according to the paint manufacturer's instructions.

6 Install casters on the bottom of the cabinet carcass so that it can be moved around the kitchen and repositioned as needed. Alternatively, you can make the cabinet into a kitchen island by anchoring it to the floor.

7 Complete the cabinet. Reattach the hardware or install new. Add decorative drawer pulls for an eye-catching accent. Reinstall the cabinet doors, making sure that they close correctly and hang level and plumb.

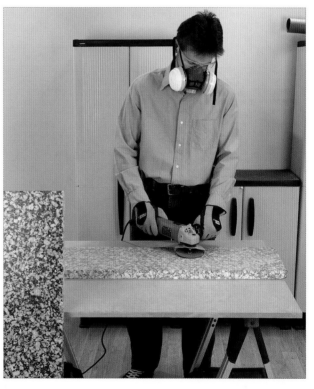

8 Clean up and rehabilitate the salvaged countertop. Here, two 12"-wide strips of 1½" thick granite are seamed together to create the countertop. Before installation, the top surface and edges of each strip are polished with an angle grinder equipped with a diamond wheel. Wear a respirator, eye and ear protection, and work in a well-ventilated area.

9 Position one countertop strip on the cabinet with the overhangs roughly equal at the sides. Apply a bead of clear polyurethane sealant to the mating edge of the first strip.

10 Place the second strip on the cabinet and press it firmly against the first. Use bar or pipe clamps to hold the strips together.

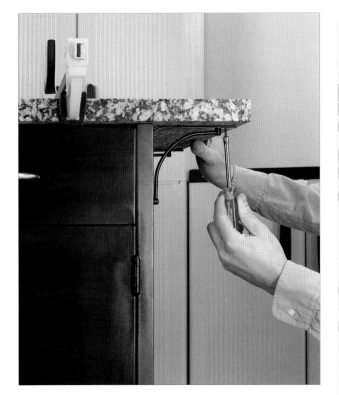

11 Anchor the countertop to the mounting brackets. Use a masonry bit to drill holes in the underside of the countertop, to accept masonry screws. Apply a few drops of epoxy into each screw hole before fastening the brackets to the countertops.

SALVAGE WISDOM: STONE ODDS AND ENDS

Small projects such as this cabinet top are ideal uses of reclaimed stone. Although you may sometimes find large sections of reclaimed granite or marble that will provide all the surface area you need for an entire kitchen's worth of countertops, more often than not, you'll be faced with smaller sections and mismatched pieces. You can use these for islands, or incorporate them as an accent section as part of a longer run of countertops in a complementary material such as Corian. You can also cut and polish pieces to make large cutting boards or incredibly beautiful sideboard hot plate trivets.

WORKING WITH LOOSE STONE

Stone has many faces, and although the finer varieties such as travertine, slate, and marble tend to get the most attention, they are hardly the only types commonly reclaimed. In fact, whether you're deconstructing an old barn or strolling the aisles at a salvage company, you are far more likely to come upon less prestigious loose stones. These include fieldstones and flagstones unearthed from local meadows and excavations, and pavers either reclaimed when sidewalks or old streets are redone, or left over from backyard pathway projects. Although they aren't as prized for their appearances as their quarried cousins might be, loose stones are less expensive, more plentiful, and easier to work with.

They can also be easy to reclaim. Flagstone was often dry stacked, which means no mortar holds the stones in place. Cobblestone and other pavers are usually laid in a bed of soil and firmed down with sand—so they can be salvaged with little more than a shovel and some hard work.

The original uses reflect the rugged nature of loose stone. They are the workhorses among natural building materials, the stuff of which foundations are often made. You'll find loose stones holding up barns, or

Flagstones are plentiful, inexpensive, easy to work with, and ruggedly handsome.

comprising the entire walls of much older structures. They were also widely used as dry-laid property walls separating one area from another. Occasionally they were pressed into service as flooring, but there are too many more impressive modern options for that to be the case today. However, loose stones were often used to create fireplace structures, which remains one of the best uses for reclaimed loose stone.

Working with these materials is easier than adapting finer stone surfaces to your purposes. A material such as fieldstone is forgiving of imprecision, and granite pavers can be used without the fine cuts you would need for a marble countertop. The most laborious part of working with loose stones is usually lifting, cleaning, and prepping them for re-use.

Although they tend to look very rustic, loose stones aren't just for log cabins and lodges set deep in the woods. A stacked flagstone fireplace surround is impressive in just about any style of home. It can also be used for low divider walls and, in recent years, has seen exposure as fronting for accent walls. Pavers can be reused to make outdoor paths, but they can also make unique floors for a bathroom or impressive steps in a mudroom, walls, or even used—as shown here—to make fireplace surrounds. Indeed, the stones are adaptable far beyond their pioneer roots; it's just a matter of looking beyond the rugged nature of the material.

Cast concrete pavers come in many sizes, shapes, and colors for creative projects inside or outside the house.

Leftover pavers from a patio project are stacked to create a surround for an electric fireplace insert.

BUILDING A PAVER FIREPLACE SURROUND

The trick in using pavers to their best advantage is to make use of the combined power of form, texture, and color. A stacked surface such as this creates interesting and regular lines in the courses, as well as an undulating surface texture that invites touching. Paver colors range from grey to red to cream and beyond and add an understated touch to any room. The chances are, if you've purchased or reclaimed the pavers as a complete lot, coloring is going to be uniform throughout. You should check anyway just to be sure, and if there is significant color variation between stones, spend some time deciding on what stones will go where for the best visual impression.

In any case, this style of fireplace surround is a fairly traditional look, and one that works every bit as well in a contemporary home as it would in a cabin or A-frame ski lodge. Add to that adaptability the fact that the surface is actually fairly easy and quick to install. It should take you less than a day. This particular project was just a bit more involved because we installed a new electric fireplace in the wall. These types of fireplaces can go right into a drywall cavity; there is no real fire and the fireplace needs no special venting or complicated insulation.

The project here was done against a sheetrocked wall, making the installation straightforward, and the surround was built to half height. The look serves as a perfect foil for the aftermarket fireplace, and the combination transforms the wall and the room. For a more dramatic appearance, stack a stone or paved surround up to the ceiling. We've added two stone mantels. But many people choose to use a weathered, reclaimed timber. It's a matter of taste, but if you're going to stack the surround any higher, it's wise to sandwich the mantel in the middle of the structure regardless of whether you're bolting it to the wall or mortaring it to the stone. Although this paver construction will be stable in and of itself using the methods described, mounting anything on the front of the stone could stress and compromise the structure.

The pavers used for this project are new masonry units left over from a patio installation. You could also salvage old sand-set or dry-set pavers, but if you have pavers that were set in mortar they're probably not worth using in an indoor installation.

(Continued)

1 Measure the area for the surround and the fireplace dimensions. Determine the exact top of the fireplace, because you'll be setting a support slab across both sides of the surround to complete it. Dry stack the pavers to ensure that you have enough of them to cover the area entirely. Mask off the floor to protect it.

2 After you've dry laid the stone up to the support slab, check the fit of the electric fireplace by sliding it into the hole in the surround and holding it up against the wall. Once you're satisfied, mark the wall for the fireplace opening.

Turn off power before cutting into wall.

3 Use a drywall or a keyhole saw to cut the opening for the fireplace unit. Install the unit according to the manufacturer's instructions; different fireplaces use different mounting methods. Most electric fireplaces have a power cord and plug. This unit was hard wired into the wall. *Note: In many instances you will need to cut wall studs to complete this project. Do not cut studs in load-bearing walls, however, and be sure to consult an engineer or building inspector for instructions on providing temporary or permanent support.*

4 Re-lay the first row of pavers and check for level. Usually, pavers are fairly uniform, although you may encounter one or more that are odd sizes. Adjust the courses as necessary to accommodate for any unusual pavers (or replace the paver). Mark wall stud locations

5 Use a caulk gun to lay a generous bed of construction adhesive labeled for use on masonry. Keep the bead of adhesive at least an inch from the front of the pavers so that you maintain a dry-laid look.

6 Every few courses, screw L brackets into the studs on either side of the fireplace and bed the legs of the brackets in the construction adhesive between courses.

7 Check level for each course as you work and adjust as necessary. When you get to the top of the fireplace, check level from side to side and use different pavers if necessary to create a perfectly level mounting surface for the support mantel.

8 Dry lay the top support slab and check for level. Once you're satisfied with the fit and look, remove the slab, cover the top course of pavers in adhesive, and re-set the slab in place. Let the adhesive set before continuing.

9 Lay paver courses on top of the support slab. For the project here, we laid a roughly equal height of pavers above and below the fireplace, although you can adjust the location of the fireplace and courses for a more asymmetrical look if desired.

RECLAIMING KILN-FIRED MATERIALS

It is the natural materials, the hand-hewn, vividly grained timber and darkly captivating black slate, that draw the most attention when a building is torn apart. But man-made pieces, in the form of kiln-fired tiles and bricks, can be every bit as alluring and useful. In fact, some of the most dramatic decorative elements you might rescue from a building are those that were born in a fire.

Kiln-fired materials such as building brick and terra cotta tiles are likely to be some of the most structurally intact pieces of a building (as long as the process of deconstruction itself has not resulted in their purposeful destruction). Bricks have been used for centuries in this country because of their structural integrity, fire resistance, and natural beauty. In Europe, terra cotta has been included in buildings dating back a millennium or more. And still they endure.

Bricks are the most commonly reclaimed kiln-fired materials. Bricks became popular as a structural building material in the early 1900s, due primarily to their innate fire-resistance. Because they were so easy to build with and are structurally sound and impervious to burning, they were used widely in valuable properties such as factories, textile mills, and large barns as well as public and commercial inner-city buildings meant to stand the test of time. They were generally used to form the walls, but builders didn't stop there. Certain types of bricks were used to pave streets, walkways, and private driveways in many parts of the country. Although the vast majority of these surfaces have either been dug up or paved over, the bricks from many of them live on in salvage company warehouses.

Many of the antique bricks you will reclaim, or that are available on the market, were manufactured by hand. The exact processes differed region to region and manufacturer to manufacturer. This makes for a lot of variation in reclaimed brick size and appearance. The bricks were also often marked with a manufacturing stamp, such as the name of the maker or, in the case of many antique bricks manufactured in Chicago, the words "union made." Colors range from the familiar bright red to black. Certain colors are indicative of a type of manufacturing or use. For instance, antique fire bricks that were used to line the fireboxes of residential fireplaces are often yellow or cream colored, with fascinating variations as a result of long exposure to extreme temperatures. Textures are similarly varied. Brick can be found with rough course surfaces or nearly smooth faces. But even given the differences in manufacturing

processes, these bricks have often lasted 100 years or more, and could quite possibly last another 100.

Terra cotta tiles are a fairly recent home decor addition in the United States, but they have been a common fixture in the floors, countertops, and patios of Europe for over a thousand years. That's why most of the reclaimed terra cotta tile available now is imported from Europe. It's every bit as enchanting as you might expect of a material that adorned Roman villas. Just like antique brick, the firing method and clay composition used to make the tiles influences how they look. Bits of straw and other debris are sometimes apparent, but not in a detrimental fashion.

The physical appearance of these tiles has been tempered by their long use, abundant sun, and the occasional wine spill. The finish, coated as it is with the residue of countless dinner fires and the bottom of sandals, has an intriguing visual depth. The colors range from creamy off-white to yellow, dusty red and deep purple to almost black. The tones are exceedingly rich.

Antique terra cotta tiles are even less regimented in format than old brick is (although many suppliers cut them down to uniform sizes). The tiles come in a variety of distinctive shapes, but the most prevalent are square, rectangular, diamond, and octagon. The actual

These antique square European terra cotta tiles are rich with a history that is reflected in the well worn surfaces and variegated colors. The tiles are well suited for duty as flooring, backsplashes, and even tub and tile surrounds.

size of the tiles varies not only place to place, but also in tiles from the same location. They will differ slightly in width, but can differ even more in thickness, because both the manufacturing and laying of the tile were done completely by hand. Some were stamped or etched with insignia, such as initials or family crests, while others were marked with standard designs of the time, such as fleur-de-lis. The styles, size and coloring also differ greatly depending from country to country, and even within a given country. For instance, antique terra cotta tile from Italy's Tuscan region is visibly different from antique tiles reclaimed from the vicinity of Rome. Terra cotta roofing tiles are also sometimes reclaimed, but their use is limited given the unusual arcing shape.

Regardless of where they come from or what appearance they boast, terra cotta tiles must be carefully installed and sealed. The surface is prone to problems such as efflorescence if not properly treated. However, most suppliers of terra cotta tile also supply formulas for treating the surface, as well as detailed instructions for proper installation.

Reclaimed ceramic tile is somewhat easier to work with, although significantly more fragile. Truly antique varieties can be spectacular examples of handcrafted artistry and are rarities. Tiles from early America as well as those from Europe—dating from the 1600s to 1900s—are one-of-a-kind pieces that carry the price tag and allure of other true antiques. Given the expense (a single tile can run hundreds of dollars), these are

Antique ceramic tiles were often painted to form intricate and enchanting large-field designs.

usually only used as accents in a decorative tile scheme that won't see use as a work surface. However, salvagers regularly reclaim ceramic tiles of more recent vintage. But even though the tiles may not be hand painted, they do often feature a patina of age, such as whites that have mellowed into a creamy yellow, and many include machine stamped designs that will have degraded in intriguing ways.

Terra cotta roofing tiles are often reclaimed and can be used in many decorative ways.

TYPES OF RECLAIMED BRICK

Before brick-making became a largely mechanical and automated process, the quality and character of any given batch of bricks varied in the extreme. In addition, different bricks were—and are—used for different applications. Bricks that would comprise the substructure of a building did not need to be weatherproof or particularly attractive, while the face brick that formed the facade of a building like a bank had to be both. Early manufacturing processes were variable. The look and integrity of any given batch of bricks depended on the quality of materials (which could change given irregular supply), the abilities of the workers, the speed at which the bricks needed to be produced, and even where the bricks were positioned in the kiln. But all bricks—reclaimed or new—are broken down into general classifications according to the intended use.

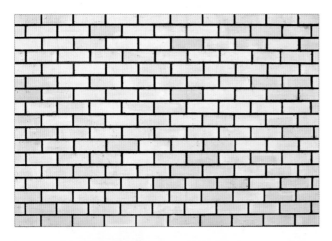

COMMON, OR BUILDING

As the name might suggest, common bricks—also known as building bricks—were meant as workhorse units. In general, they are not considered the most beautiful bricks and appearance was secondary to structural performance. Although intended for functional uses, common bricks were often used as facing brick when a lack of facing brick might have held up construction of a building. This was generally done on cruder buildings where appearance was not a major concern. Used in exterior facing applications, many common bricks would fail; spalding was a regular problem. However, defective bricks are not usually reclaimed, so the common bricks rescued during renovations or deconstruction are likely to be extremely sound. More modern types of common bricks include frogged, which are manufactured with indentations, and perforated, which can have many small or a few large holes through the brick. These are lesser forms and are usually not reclaimed.

FACE BRICK

Antique face brick can be a valuable reclaimed material because color, texture, and size are all more uniform than with other types of antique brick. The face brick was usually the best of any given lot, and was manufactured to stand up to moisture and the elements and still maintain its attractive appearance. The look is usually indicative of a given region, and these can be some of the most beautiful bricks. Even more recent face bricks are well worth the effort of reclaiming them.

PAVING

These bricks were specifically formulated to withstand the abuse of traffic and the elements. If you're considering putting in a pathway, patio, or driveway, you should always select bricks designated as pavers. Common bricks will generally not hold up to freeze-thaw cycles in areas of the country where the ground freezes, and you should never use a frogged or holed brick for paving purposes. Pavers were also made to resist moisture infiltration, even when kept wet for long periods. They have proven their longevity not only over time, but through exceptional wear and tear—they were used as the road paving material of choice from the introduction of the automobile in the first decade of the 20th century through the development of asphalt in the 1930s. In fact, quality paver bricks are the equal to granite cobblestones. There are many different types of antique brick pavers available, from standard rectangles to interlocking "keystone" bricks. Reclaimed and salvaged pavers often have a lovely worn smooth side. The colors are deeper than modern bricks, and antique bricks do not fade over time or under the glare of sun exposure. Like most bricks, the look, size and shape of antique pavers are usually unique to the region in which they were made and laid. Many companies offer pavers by geographic designation, such as Chicago pavers.

CLINKER

Clinkers are some of the most unusual, interesting, and downright fun bricks to use. Formed in the hottest areas of the kiln, their location resulted in odd colors and often distorted shapes. Clinkers were at first considered waste bricks and discarded. They actually were named for the distinctive almost metallic sound they made when thrown onto the waste pile. But in the 1920s, craftsman realized that these bricks were special and could be used in special ways. Dark purple and black bricks were incorporated into the face of walls on commercial buildings to spell out the initials or simple logos of the company that owned the building. Misshapen clinkers were included in exterior walls to create unorthodox and incredibly interesting flowing designs. Clinkers are, by the nature of their production, harder, heavier and denser than other bricks, making them very resistant to moisture and wear. They can be incorporated into exterior applications including walls, benches, and pathways, but they also add something special to indoor applications such as fireplace surrounds. And the exacting tolerances of modern manufacturing methods ensures that the existing clinkers are all that will ever be made.

FIREBRICK

Although in a more general sense, firebricks are any that are used to line ovens, kilns, and fireplaces, the reclaimed firebricks or those found at salvage shops are the ones used to line the fireboxes of residential fireplaces. These bricks were specially designed to withstand extremely high temperatures. The manufacturing process created firebricks in many captivating colors, including cream,

grey, red, yellow, tan, and black. As if the original color range was not interesting enough, exposure to open flame over decades or a century or more added scintillating depth to these colors, altering the hues and creating patinas that can't be found in any other brick type. Firebricks are best reused in fireplace designs, although they can be used in other projects as well.

RECLAIMING & CLEANING BRICK

You can reclaim brick from exterior walls or interior locations such as a fireplace surround with just a little hard work. Use a pneumatic hammer with a blade bit on the mortar joint between bricks. Older brick was mortared with limestone mortar, which is softer than modern cement mortar. Work from the top down to remove bricks, and expect that 10 percent of the bricks may be destroyed in the process. Don't concern yourself with removing all of the mortar while you're excavating bricks from a wall—that is part of the following clean-up process.

Removing bricks from a mortared location raises a lot of dust, and can make a lot of noise. Always wear appropriate eye protection, ear protection, and a dust mask. To dull the vibration of the pneumatic hammer, it's wise to wear a quality pair of thick work gloves. Work boots are also a good idea, because the bricks tend to fall before you can catch them.

As with other reclaimed materials, cleaning up salvaged brick is a sequential process in which you use the least severe methods first, moving on to the more serious processes only when you have to.

Physical removal of mortar is the place to start. Lime-based mortar is often degraded enough to make removal less of a chore than it might otherwise be. A long soak in a strong vinegar solution can also loosen mortar on bricks in many cases. You can use pure vinegar but be aware that the same dangers (albeit to a lesser degree) exist with a strong vinegar solution as with any other acidic solution.

If all else fails and you are considering the brick for a purely decorative purpose, you might consider using a wet saw or grinder to cut the most attractive face off the brick. This type of brick "veneer" has been used throughout history to create the illusion of brick wall over other surfaces. You can use it to the same effect in installations such as fireplace surrounds.

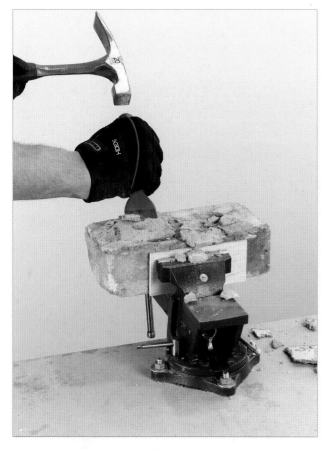

Chisel large sections of mortar off the brick, using a small cold chisel with a fine blade and a hammer. Secure the brick in a vise with padded jaws, and work slowly and carefully to avoid damaging the brick.

Use a power drill equipped with a wire wheel attachment, or a wire wheel on a bench grinder to remove the remaining mortar debris.

SALVAGE WISDOM

Stubborn mortar residue can also be removed by soaking the brick in an acidic mortar removal formula available from hardware stores, or a 10-percent muriatic acid solution (1 part acid to 10 parts water). However, muriatic acid is an extremely dangerous substance (a form of hydrochloric acid) and you must use all safety precautions recommended by the manufacturer. Start by removing as much of the mortar as possible with a chisel and hammer. Make sure you wear all necessary safety gear, including rubber gloves that go as far up the arm as possible, acid-resistant safety eyewear, and a respirator. Work outside or in a room with very strong ventilation. Set up an acid bath in a plastic or glass tub and carefully add the acid into the water—never the other way around. Then soak the brick with water before placing it in the muriatic solution. The acid usually bubbles as it goes to work on the mortar. Allow the acid to work on the mortar for about 10 minutes, then use a stiff scrub brush to brush the mortar off the brick, brushing away from your face and body. Neutralize or otherwise remove any chemical formulation you've used on the brick once you've removed the mortar. Baking soda can neutralize many acidic formulations—you just add the baking soda to the mix. Once neutralized, rinse the solution off the brick thoroughly with copious amounts of water and scrub it with a scrub brush and a mild dish soap and water solution. Allow bricks to dry completely before using them.

Chapter 5

—⁓—

RECLAIMING GLASS

In possibly no other building material is the difference between old and new more marked than it is with glass. A timeworn mirror will have lost some of its "silvering" and gained some charm, intermingling the reflected image with scars from the lost backing. Antique windows proudly bear the liquid imperfections caused by earlier crude manufacturing methods; the swirls, bubbles, and striations are endlessly engaging. A rescued beveled cabinet door lite bears elegant witness to a handcraft that is dying and disappearing. In all its many forms, reclaimed glass is something special, beautiful, and inevitably unique.

RECLAIMED WINDOW TYPES

There are many different types of windows. Some have historical precedent, and others are fairly modern innovations. Most are defined by the way they are opened and closed (or not) and each can serve a different decorative reuse. The window you choose will depend on exactly what project you have in mind and, to some degree, what type is available.

FIXED

Many—if not the majority—of reclaimed windows are this style, which consists of a basic frame, often with muntins separating different panes into what are called "divided lites." Operable windows required technology that was simply not available to the builders of many early 20th-century homes and business buildings. To owners of industrial buildings throughout the 19th and early 20th centuries, windows that opened were an unnecessary expense. But as plain as this style may sound, there is still a good deal of diversity within the category of fixed windows. For instance, antique fixed windows were regularly manufactured with frames of non-wood materials. Copper and other metal frames make for a very interesting look that can accent other decorative elements in your interior design. Home-owners that use these windows often leave the frames in their original condition, covered with the patina of age. Even framed in wood, an older fixed window can feature a lovely distressed look. The simplicity of a design with no moving parts makes these windows ideal for reuse in home design, as interior windows, tabletops, and beyond.

SINGLE OR DOUBLE-HUNG

These common styles are still used today. Featuring top and bottom sashes in which one or both slide up and down (single or double respectively), the windows can easily be taken apart so that each sash can be used separately. A fashionable trend in recent years has been to use one sash with divided lites as a wall-mounted frame for photos. A sash can also be used to create a shadow box for collectibles or other items you want to display. Older single and double-hung windows were not standardized. The size you find on a deconstruction site or at a reseller's shop may be unique and not well suited to replace an existing window. However, many newer models in standard sizes are becoming available as late-20th-century homes are being taken down and reclaimed. Because of the hidden mechanism of

counterweights, these windows are fairly difficult to reclaim yourself. It's usually wiser to buy them from a salvage source.

CASEMENT

Casement windows open from one side just as a door does, and are usually a single pane of glass. This type of window is less popular than others for a number of reasons, and it's a hard window to reuse for anything but a direct replacement of an existing failed unit. A steel-framed casement window can be separated from the jamb and opening unit to be used as a coffee table top, but other re-uses in home design are limited.

AWNING AND HOPPER

Generally smaller in size than other windows, awning and hopper windows are intriguing styles that can, in certain instances, change the look of an interior. The awning window opens from the bottom like an awning, while the hopper is just the opposite—hinged on the bottom to open like a hopper drawer. These styles can be used to great effect as over-door transom windows in a home. They can be used purely as decoration, or as conduits for extra light and airflow throughout the home. Awning windows are sometimes installed as interior wall windows, kept closed most of the time, but open when air circulation is needed. Either style is sometimes used over a curio or shadow-box table or cabinet, where the opening mechanism allows easy access.

JALOUSIE

The jalousie window was originally intended as a tropical style that could open to allow air circulation and at the same time prevent rain from entering through the window. The window is actually a set of horizontal glass "louvers" that are cranked open and shut. The style is associated with mid-20th-century architecture, and retrofitting an existing window opening with a jalousie window can add flavor to the look of a home, both inside and out. Frosted glass versions are wonderful replacements for bathroom windows because they can be opened for ventilation while maintaining privacy. Jalousie windows are most often used as replacements because of their architectural interest, but they are sometimes mounted on walls for an interesting sculptural effect. With a little imagination, the intriguing form of a jalousie can be used in home design in a number of different ways.

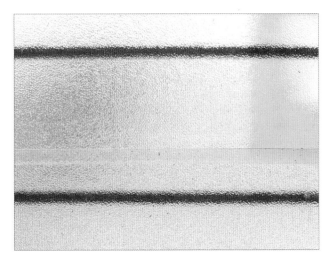

EYEBROW

Eyebrow windows are arched designs that are usually fixed but occasionally operable. The interesting shape makes a wonderful interior transom window, one that is appropriate for many different home styles. It's also a great choice for a window in a partition wall. Antique versions often feature elaborate frames, such as starburst or spiderweb designs, dividing the window up into tiny segments of glass. The frames are sometimes iron or other metal, adding to the allure of the window. When the frame is ornate, distressed, or otherwise distinctive, eyebrows can be fascinating decorative features all by themselves. Simply set atop cabinets or even bookshelves, the window draws attention. The shape lends itself to interior installation, such as at the top of a wall bordering an interior room with no exterior exposure.

PORTAL

Portals are some of the most unusual windows you can reclaim. Completely round, these windows are often salvaged from ships, and are consequently framed in brass, copper, or other metal. But even framed in bent wood, they are enchanting. The round shape brings an uncommon element to any interior, and portal windows with detailed frames and attached fixtures such as hinges or latches are often displayed on a wall all by themselves. Non-operable portal windows look incredible when installed in a solid-core door or, in a set, along an interior wall. The round shape also lends itself to a

second life as a table. Find one with antique or textured glass in the opening, and the table will likely serve as a conversation-starting centerpiece. Because they have traditionally been used more on ships than in houses, you can find the largest selection from firms specializing in marine salvage.

SALVAGED ART GLASS

Decorative glass treatments have been part of this country's history since the very first buildings were constructed. Stained glass has been a staple of churches not only here, but throughout the world. But that's just the tip of the iceberg. The Victorian period saw an explosion of both plain leaded glass windows, and stained glass in homes and other buildings. Beveled glass designs have been around for almost as long. More recently, sandblasted glass has played an increasingly prominent role in buildings both residential and corporate. Consequently, you may find decorative art glass in a building under deconstruction, but there is a huge selection among salvage firms and antique dealers. Given the range of styles that are available, you should be able to find a piece of art glass that's just right for your home with just a little searching.

LEADED

The term leaded is somewhat misleading, because most art glass—stained and beveled included—is technically "leaded." But in most cases, the phrase refers to the fact that individual pieces of glass within the window's borders are held in place by lead channels (they have a U or H in profile) called "came." Leaded windows are comprised of plain glass cut into decorative shapes and assembled into an overall design. The lead channels are soldered together

to hold the design in place, and then anchored inside the actual window frame. In general, this means that leaded windows can't be resized. But depending on the design and how much it excites your inner designer, creating a space to accommodate a leaded glass window can be well worth the effort. The designs themselves range from simple squares and rectangles to much more ornate shapes and figures. Leaded glass windows come in all shapes and sizes because they were, until fairly recently, custom made. They are not installed in operable windows, but you can replace a fixed window that is larger than a leaded glass unit by building out a frame in the opening to accommodate the smaller leaded-glass window. Some designs are so detailed and eye-catching that people mount the window on a wall by itself, although they can also be used as glass fronts for cabinets or intriguing tabletops.

STAINED GLASS

Few reclaimed architectural artifacts are as steeped in history as stained glass windows. The art of stained glass has been around for centuries, although the windows that you're likely to reclaim will probably be a few decades old at best. Regardless of age, stained glass designs range from kitsch to sublime. Even if you're not a fan of the stereotypical intensely figural designs that most people think of when they think of stained glass windows, take heart. You can find purely geometric treatments and very simple designs that are nothing more than a combination of squares and rectangles in one or two colors. The colored glass itself is fascinating. Crafted in almost every color imaginable, stained glass does not fade or wear away—the pigment is an integral part of the glass. However, vintage stained glass windows—especially any used in exterior applications—can literally fall to pieces. If you find one you like, check for bowing or gaps between the lead channels and the glass pieces, and inspect for any cracks or checking in the glass. A modestly worn stained glass window is easy to repair, but more extensive damage calls for professional help and may rule the window out. In addition to actual stained glass, you'll also find samples of painted glass windows. Artists have long painted on stained glass as they would on a canvas to create more lifelike scenes than could be crafted with the glass colors alone. The effect can be marvelous, and light passing through a painted stained glass window will be muted in dramatic dusky jewel tones. Used in the right location (one that receives significant direct natural light), a painted window can be stunning. But both stained and painted windows are best used in moderation; a single small window can create a showpiece. They can be installed in existing window openings just as a leaded window would be. A stained glass window can also make a stunning work of wall-mounted art if placed in a frame with backlighting. Smaller panels are vibrant additions to kitchen cabinets or transoms. The windows can also make amazing tables sandwiched between two pieces of tempered glass and edge banded with wood or metal to form a flat surface.

SANDBLASTED

Sandblasted, or frosted, glass is a more contemporary version of art glass. Artists use thick blast-resistant stencils to etch designs into windows, glass walls, or onto mirrors. As with other forms of art glass, sandblasted designs can be cheesy, sophisticated, and everything in between. The decorated surface permits light to shine through, while serving as a privacy screen. Solid frosted windows and other glass surfaces can be reused as short partition walls, tabletops, counters, and sidelites for interior or exterior doors. Sandblasted windows really come to life when the window can be viewed at different angles and is lit by both artificial and natural light sources.

BEVELED

The art of beveling an edge onto a thin piece of glass takes skill and well-calibrated machinery. But before technology and automation became prevalent, beveling was strictly a handcraft that required talent and a breadth of knowledge. Most antique beveled windows were made by hand, and the craftsmanship is blatantly obvious. Craftsmen lay an edge angled to make the most out of light passing through the glass. The right bevel creates a brilliant sparkle and a prismatic effect that breaks sunlight apart into a rainbow of colors. Floral designs from the early decades of the 20th century complement fussier architecture, such as Victorian homes. More geometric designs provide a pleasing linear simplicity that is appropriate for modern, contemporary, traditional and craftsman-style interiors. Beveled inserts are at home in exterior windows where the play of sunlight creates color bursts throughout the day, and in cabinet doors, where the natural sparkle improves the look of whatever is kept inside the cabinet. Like other glass art, beveled designs are held together with lead channels that are subject to the stresses of age. This is something to consider before putting a beveled panel in a structurally stressful location such as the door lite for a front door.

VINTAGE SPECIALTY GLASSES

Study antique glass panes closely and you'll probably find intriguing imperfections. Bubbles, thick areas, and streaks are all part of what was once a very imprecise production process. They are also flaws that are beautiful and desirable. But as glassmakers became more proficient and exacting in how they made glass, they realized they could control the process to make uniform the flaws that were once accidental. The result were specialty glasses, a variety of textures that were either purposely imprinted on the molten glass surface to create stunning, clear glass patterns, or manipulated into the form of the glass to create body and life in the forever frozen material. Originally used primarily to create privacy without reducing light transmission, these glasses have become decorative pieces in their own right.

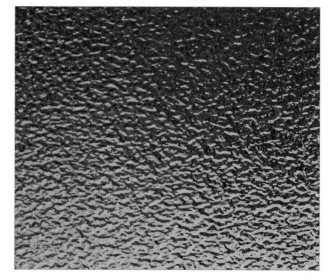

TEXTURED

The process is fairly simple and mechanical, which is why textured glasses are sometimes referred to as "machined" glass. Right after the hot sheets of glass are formed, a steel form or stencil imprints the surface with a texture. The texture can be random or, more often, it is regular and standardized. Textured glasses are still made today, but many of the patterns available through salvagers are unique. Panes of textured glass are most at home where privacy is needed, such as a bathroom door or window. But they can bring exciting touches to the doors on cabinets of any type. It's a way of having glass-fronted cabinet doors without worrying if what's in the cabinet is worth showing. Textured glass is fairly easy to cut, so panes can usually be resized to fit any opening.

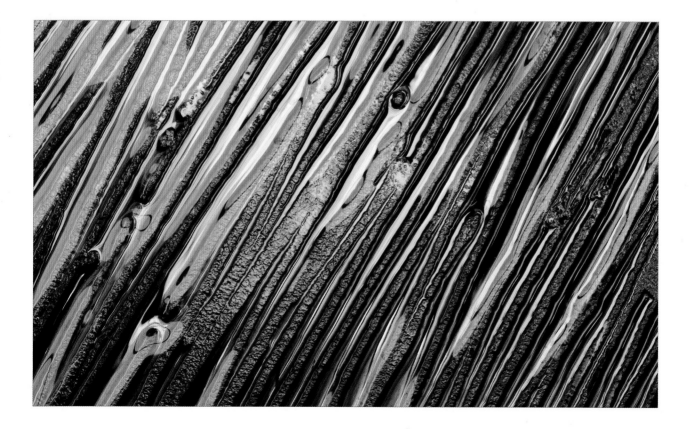

SPECIALTY GLASSES

The same companies that produced stained glass used a similar process to form clear specialty glasses in a range of styles. These are often named for the visual effect, such as "water glass" that looks like flowing water, and "seedy," which looks as if clear seeds have been embedded in the glass. The effects are incredibly varied and the patterns are often unique. Depending on what form the glass was given, it may entirely obscure a view, partially obscure, or simply add wrinkles to what you see. Like machine-textured glasses, these types can be cut and resized for use as tabletops, replacement windowpanes, door and sidelites, and more. They can even be painted white on one side and used as backsplash tiles.

INDUSTRIAL GLASS

Chicken wire glass is a specialty glass that was regularly used in industrial settings. The glass is formed with wire inside it to prevent shattering, and the surface was often textured as well. The glass was specially made in the ages before tempered glass to add security and ensure against breakage. The design also prevented injury; if broken, large pieces of sharp glass would be held in place by the wire. Because it was used primarily in industrial settings, chicken wire glass is often framed in sturdy, industrial metal framing. The framing itself can be visually arresting, and the combination makes for a focal point replacement window. Chicken wire glass is almost exclusively available in fixed-window form, and can't easily be cut down to size or modified. But large panels are used as room dividers, shower doors, or windows. Some are sturdy enough to be used as dining room tables or desks. Corrugated glass is similar to chicken wire glass, in that it was used in factories as a strong and safe transparent surface—usually for awnings, roofs, or skylights. Corrugated glass panels are generally large, with the rippled form you would expect from the name. The panels can be professionally cut down to form fronts for breakfast bars, half-height divider walls, and other sculptural uses.

REVIVING A RECLAIMED WINDOW

1 Remove all the old putty from around the panes of glass and remove any cracked or broken panes entirely. You can use linseed oil applied and left for an hour or so to soften old putty, or use a heat gun. Move the gun slowly and continually along the putty line.

2 Using a putty knife, pry out the old putty as soon as it softens. Scrape the glass channel clean, removing all the old putty and dirt, but take care not to gouge the window's wood. Use needlenose pliers to pull out any glazing points left in the channel after you've removed the putty.

3 Sand lightly as necessary to clean out any stubborn putty. Once the glass opening is completely cleaned, prime the surface for the wood putty by brushing on a coat of linseed oil or primer. If the wood isn't sealed, the dry surface will draw moisture from the putty, compromising the final glass seal.

4 Roll a thin bead of putty to about the diameter of a chopstick, and line the channel. Smooth it in place with your thumb.

(Continued)

5 Clean the glass—especially the edges so they will seal with the putty—and lay the pane in the putty bed. Use gloves to avoid cuts and smears on the glass, and press the pane lightly but firmly down. Wiggle the pane slightly from side to side as you press down, until it is completely seated.

6 Drive glazier's points into the wood frame to hold the pane in place. Use the tip of the putty knife to slide the point into position against the pane and into the wood frame. Use at least 2 points on each side of the pane.

7 Roll a rope of putty and press it along the seam between wood and glass. Push the putty down into place and create a neat beveled edge by dragging along a putty knife held at a 45° angle. Remove any excess putty.

8 Let the putty dry for several days until it is no longer cool to the touch. Prime and paint the sash and over the putty bead. Paint onto the glass to ensure a good seal and scrape off the excess paint with a razor.

CUTTING RECLAIMED GLASS

1 Clean the glass thoroughly. Place the glass on a clean, flat, and level surface. The surface should be rubber or other material that will prevent the glass from sliding as you apply pressure. Textured glasses normally have a smooth side, opposite the textured side. Cut the smooth side.

2 Mark the cut line along the glass. Use a metal straight edge, one that is thick enough to avoid catching the cutter's wheel, and align it along the cut line.

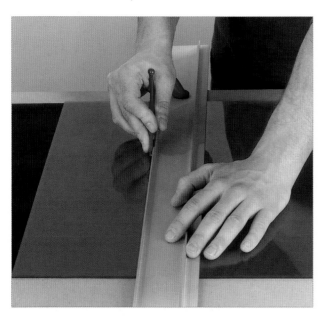

3 Dip the cutter's wheel in light oil or fill the oil reservoir. Tuck the handle between the index and middle fingers, with the point of your thumb bracing the underside of the handle. Hold the cutter at a slight angle and press down with firm pressure. Draw the cutter along the straight edge toward you, in one smooth motion.

4 Hold the pane of glass along the edge of a table or scrap piece of wood so that the cut line is aligned with the edge of the underlying surface. Placing a hand on either side of the glass as you would hold a newspaper; snap both ends down. If the glass doesn't easily break, tap along the cutting line with the breaking ball on the end of the cutter's handle.

BUILD A RECLAIMED WINDOW CABINET

There are many uses for reclaimed windows in the home. Although the most obvious is simply to install an antique window into an existing opening, you might want to turn to more creative options. Few uses are as charming and practical as the window cabinet described here. It's not just the allure of a distressed or obviously older window. Although that can certainly be a draw, the real attraction of this particular design is that it is so adaptable. The construction of the cabinet body is easy enough that anyone with basic woodworking skills and some fundamental tools can put the whole thing together in about a day. You can also use just about any window you find (round windows won't work) and alter the dimensions to suit the window. A small transom window, for instance,

could be used for a bathroom toiletries cabinet. Use two windows to make a dual-compartment cabinet. A long, thin window can be positioned sideways to make a low-slung media center cabinet. And the options don't stop at your choice of window.

We've used reclaimed lumber for this carcass, something you might want to consider if you want to carry through the whole reclaimed ideal—and if you want to create a unique look in the wood carcass that supports the window. Of course, whether the wood is reclaimed or you use some pieces you have lying around the garage, you can choose a finish that suits your tastes and decor. Paint the window frame and box a bright color to fit in with your retro living room, or finish it all natural to serve as a bar cabinet in your

contemporary dining room. Between paint, stains, and clear finishes, your options are mind-boggling.

And don't forget the accents. For the cabinet shown here, we chose exposed hinges and handles that carry through the antique style. You can select copper, bronze, chrome, iron, or other hardware for just the right finishing touches on your own cabinet.

The number of shelves is up to you as well. Depending on what you intend to store in the cabinet, you may want more shelves, or you may decide to position shelves differently. We've placed one right in the middle of the cabinet and cut a slot for the shelf that mirrors the dadoes we cut for the top and bottom of the cabinet. But you could just as easily use any of a number of shelf support systems on the inside of a cabinet carcass. Many of these allow for adjustability, which again, might be your preference. And like the number of shelves, you can decide to build a freestanding cabinet as we have here, or a wall-mounted unit. Although you can clad the back in a simple 1/4" plywood sheet cut to fit the outline, we've left the back open. If you leave the back open, you can hang the cabinet by screwing it to top and side cleats that are attached to the wall or, if you add a back, you can screw the back directly to the wall. There are many other ways to hang the cabinet—a trip to the home center will yield many different possibilities. But whether you hang the cabinet or let it stand all by itself, it's sure to be an exceptional focal point in your home's design.

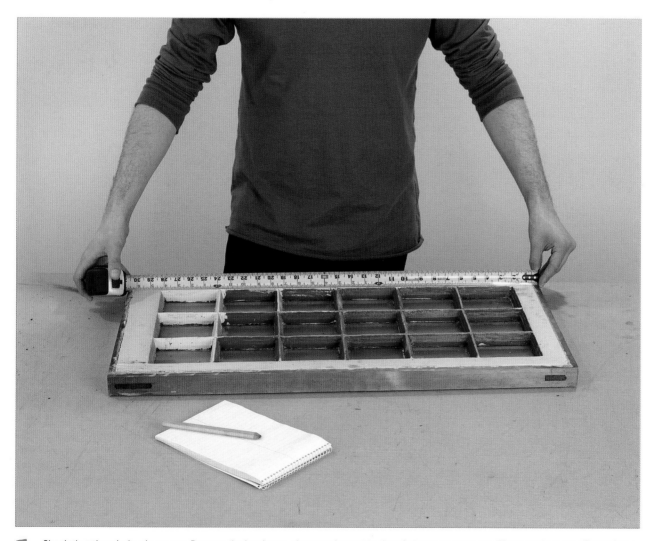

1 Check that the window is square. Remove the hardware, clean, and re-putty the window as necessary. Measure the outer dimensions of the window and note them.

(Continued)

2 Mark and cut the planks that will serve as the sides approximately 4" longer than the height of the window. This is to account for the dadoes that will hold the top and bottom, and to create top and bottom lips. If you prefer, you can cut the sides to the height of the window, and butt join the top and bottom pieces to the sides.

3 Cut the top, bottom and shelf for the unit. In this case, they each must be 1" longer than the width of the window. This will allow for 1/2" of each cross piece to rest in the dadoes on each side.

4 Carefully measure and mark each side plank so that the height of the window is centered along the length of the plank. The top and bottom dadoes will be cut just outside these marks. Use a table saw or router to cut 1/2" dadoes on the least attractive faces of the planks.

5 Assemble the cabinet carcass by sliding the top, bottom, and shelf into the side-plank dadoes. Drive finish nails through the outside faces of the sides, into the cross pieces. Use a nailset to sink the nails and putty over them.

Alternative: If the cabinet will need to support heavy weight or will be hung in a high-traffic area, use screws instead of finish nails. Pre-drill countersunk holes and attach the pieces with flathead wood screws. Plug over the screw heads with wood plugs of the same type of wood.

6 Sand and paint or stain the cabinet body and window in whatever finish you've chosen. If you're leaving reclaimed wood in its existing state and finish, seal the puttied nail heads and any bare wood surfaces with clear polyurethane.

7 Attach the hinges to the window, and position the window in place. Mark the hinge holes on the cabinet side and door hand latch on the other. Pre-drill the holes and install the window on the front of the cabinet. Hang the cabinet if desired.

Chapter 6

—⚬—

SALVAGING FIXTURES & ARCHITECTURAL ACCENTS

Many of the structures taken down each year are industrial or bare-bones rural buildings such as barns or warehouses. The materials that come from those buildings are fundamental structural elements. But many more houses are demolished or completely renovated every year, yielding a treasure chest full of non-structural fixtures and accents. These are often the perfect icing on the cake for your own home design, and can bring a bit of style from the past to perk up your present home.

Fixtures and accents salvaged from buildings being demolished, updated, or simply falling down of their own accord usually feature styling specific to a given period. But that doesn't mean you have to be a historian or know exactly what era a doorknob or light fixture comes from to incorporate it into your house. It comes down to what your tastes are and how the feature will work with the other elements in your home design. Luckily many different salvageable items can complement just about any decor or home style.

Cut glass doorknobs, simple art deco wall sconces, or a cast iron tub that is just the right shape and size to suit your bathroom remodel will all work regardless of what the rest of your home looks like. One of the wonderful things about many architectural accents is that they can stand on their own, just as a painting or photo would.

Reclaiming some of these will be a matter of need. After all, you don't just decide to swap out your bathroom sink and vanity because you happened upon a hand-painted ceramic unit from the '40s. But in other instances, you can shop with an eye to possibilities. If you have a house full of darkly stained doors, you might be open to the box full of brass doorknobs and locksets you find a local antiques shop or salvage warehouse.

TYPES OF SALVAGED FIXTURES & ACCENTS

PLUMBING FIXTURES

The vintage tubs and kitchen sinks you'll find on the reclaimed marketplace are not only uniquely styled, they are also usually made of almost indestructible enameled cast iron. Every historical period has its own style and the same is true of sinks, tubs, and toilets from those periods. Sinks are available in all the shapes you'll find today, but most are surface mounted or standalone. Original farmhouse sinks with the front apron style that is popular in today's market are a wonderful find. Older pedestal sinks can feature incredibly stylistic flourishes, such as fluted column bases, multi-tiered edge forms, and units with formed backsplashes. Both kitchen and bathroom sinks were made of porcelain and porcelain-plated cast iron. A smaller number of kitchen sinks were made of stainless steel, usually under a brand name created by the manufacturer. You'll find vintage wall-mounted and pedestal bathroom sinks and older vanity sinks. Kitchen and utility sinks were manufactured as standalone units as well, but with single or multiple bowls. Many featured very cool and useful built-in features, such as soap dishes and

drainboards with grooves that direct fluids back into the basin. Of course, there are also newer sinks on the market, reclaimed from houses built in the 1960s, or from remodeling projects. These can include stone sinks such as marble, and versions made out of engineered or synthetic materials. As a general rule, if you're going to the trouble of shopping for a reclaimed sink, the biggest reward will come in the form of an iron, metal, or high-end stone sink. Synthetic versions are less likely to hold up over time or feature distinctive styling.

Reclaimed bathtubs are available in much the same materials as period sinks are, but they come in two basic styles: apron or built-in, and freestanding (pedestal and clawfoot). Salvaged built-in tubs often feature elegant styling and shapes. Standard apron tubs slide right into a U-shaped cavity, while alcove tubs have a wraparound apron that allows them to sit in the L formed by two intersecting walls. Alcove tubs can only be positioned one way, fitting into either a right-hand or left-hand corner. Clawfoot and pedestal tubs are freestanding and can be positioned anywhere the drain can connect to the waste line. The tub can be serviced by faucets or fixtures routed up through the floor or out of a wall. Clawfoot models are some of the most impressive antique tubs, and will work with many different styles of home decor. Although pedestal tubs are somewhat more rare, they are impressive in their own right. They require a lot of floor space, but can make a powerful design statement in the right bathroom, not to mention being a luxurious place to take a bath. Many older tubs are exceptionally long or deep (or both) and provide a sumptuous bathing experience. However, these variations in size are why you need to measure carefully to ensure that you have the proper space to accommodate a reclaimed tub.

Toilets are usually reclaimed only if you're trying to re-create a true period look. Older toilets were generally six-gallon units that don't conform to modern codes or best environmental practices. Reclaimed toilets can, however, be incredible bargains if you can use them in a bathroom renovation.

Plumbing hardware includes faucets, showerheads, decorative handles, and the exposed faucet bodies used with freestanding tubs. These are stylish, often crafted in brass, steel, and copper. Their appearances, whether left aged or cleaned up to sparkle like new, separate them from the more common contemporary chrome fixtures. Faucets, spigots, and showerheads are usually rebuilt with new valves, screens, and washers. Some parts, such as the pretty ceramic handles so often re-created by modern manufacturers, can be re-used for purely decorative purposes.

COLUMNS & POSTS

Columns are part of this country's architectural heritage, and they are often reclaimed from larger and once-grand homes being deconstructed or demolished. Older columns were usually constructed of wood, although you may find structural stone, or decorative plaster columns as well (fiberglass models are more modern versions). Even if you're not ready to construct a facade worthy of columns on your home, there are many different ways to re-use these structures. They are re-purposed to create arbors on existing outdoor decks, and can be cut in half to make simple furniture such as a small table, or as supports for a breakfast bar. They can also be used as interior decoration, placed under either end of a header as faux structural supports. Even when the entire column is not reclaimed, the decorative top and bottom pieces—known as "capitals"—often are. These can serve a host of design roles in the home: as bases for low tables, or to support bookshelves, and even more decorative roles. Capitals are often incredibly ornate and beautiful, and are regularly used to great dramatic effect with the distressed appearance left by aging. Posts are more plentiful on the reclaimed marketplace and are more easily adapted to use in the home. They are available in just about every historical style from early colonial to craftsman and beyond. Posts can be repurposed as staircase newels, braces for a breakfast bar, console table, or standalone accent tables, or even as simple plant stands.

HARDWARE

Doorknobs, hinges, sash locks, cabinet hardware, and mail slots are all recovered during demolition and deconstruction. They are reused as interesting and stylish features. Doorknobs and locksets are some of the most widely recovered accents because they are so easy to adapt for use on new doors. Doorknobs are also common finds at a salvage or architectural antiques shop, and are a great way to add a distinctive touch of flair to otherwise ordinary doors. Ornament a single door, such as a front door, or buy a group of reclaimed doorknobs and replace all interior door hardware. Exterior or interior door hinges are less commonly re-used because they often don't fit your existing doors. But where they do, or where you're replacing a door with a reclaimed unit, vintage hinges can be the icing on the cake. Old cabinet hardware can also make a wonderful accent in kitchens. More elaborate or period-style hardware, or pieces crafted of unique metals or finishes, can create visual interest on otherwise mundane cabinets. In fact, the visual impact of replacing your cabinet hardware with reclaimed pieces far exceeds the modest cost. Even if a period-style latch and hinges aren't right for all the cabinets in your kitchen, you can use them to spruce up a standalone storage piece, such as a bar or hutch. Lastly, antique mail slots are conversation pieces that can be used as originally intended or for display purposes.

LIGHTING FIXTURES

Reclaimed lighting fixtures present an array of styles for the homeowner looking to install interesting interior or exterior lighting. Aside from the period-style fixtures salvaged from older homes, lighting fixtures are rescued from industrial facilities such as warehouses, public plants such as airports that are being updated, and other non-building sources such as ships that are being refitted or mothballed. The result is a salvaged lighting market rich with unusual, distinct, and fabulous options. Although these may require rewiring to update the fixture, the effort is usually well worth it. Fixtures from wall sconces to chandeliers to vintage exterior safety lights are available in metals and glasses not commonly found today, and crafted in designs that will never be executed again. That's not to say that you should only consider a reclaimed fixture if you're after an unusual look; you'll find plenty of more modest ceiling and hanging lights in simple yet attractive styles. You'll even find contemporary styles salvaged from home remodels and gutted office buildings—something to keep in mind if you're looking to closely match existing fixtures.

ARCHITECTURAL ORNAMENTS

The buildings of decades past included many architectural features that served decorative purposes (often along with structural roles), embellishing the architectural style of homes, public buildings, and commercial structures alike. These include corbels—elegantly designed brackets meant to hold up, or appear to hold up, a ceiling, beam, or other structural element. They are wonderful touches in a home when used as they originally were, although they can also make stunning brackets for shelves, fireplace mantels, or even a breakfast bar. Antique shops and salvage operations offer corbels small and large, in wood, metal, and, occasionally, even plaster. Although many manufacturers make reproduction corbels, the intricacy and unique designs of reclaimed versions far outshine what is currently available. Other brackets are regular staples of salvage company offerings, and are useful for holding up shelves of any kind. Lintels are decorative headers, sometimes adorned with a frieze or other design. Lintels are often stone, but were also crafted in wood and metal. Some are simple rectangles, while others are arched, or formed into more ornate shapes. These are less easily adapted for use in a home, and are most often used as simple display pieces to show off the handcrafted designs. Other architectural elements that can find decorative roles in the modern home include roofline cornices, gargoyles, and other mounted statuary, such as lion-face water spout outlets. These are usually used as focal points in and of themselves.

RECONDITIONING RECLAIMED PLUMBING FIXTURES

Bringing a porcelain or enameled-cast-iron sink, tub, or toilet back to life may entail finding an effective treatment for different types of stains. It's wisest to start with the mildest cleaning strategy, working your way up to more severe solutions only when the simpler treatments aren't effective. Regardless of the stains or condition of the sink, toilet, or tub you're reclaiming, always begin by thoroughly cleaning the surface with a general, non-abrasive bathroom cleaner. Once you've removed the stains and blemishes, you should always keep the surface clean with a gentle, non-abrasive cleanser and a cloth or nylon scrubber. Fix leaks immediately to avoid rust stains, and consider softening your water if your water source is a well or unconditioned city water.

RUST STAINS

Some of the most common blemishes on older enamel and porcelain surfaces, rust stains are usually not as difficult to remove as they first appear. Start with a simple home remedy—mix salt and lemon juice and spread the paste over the stain. Let it sit for several hours and then rinse thoroughly. You can also turn to a paste made of cream of tartar and water, and used in the same way as the lemon solution. If the rust stain is not completely gone, use a pumice stone or pumice paste on the rust stain. Simply rub the stone or paste over the stain until it is removed. Pumice stones and other pumice-based cleaning products are available at large home centers. Another solution is trisodium phosphate, which will be effective on many rust stains, as well as other stains. If the stain stubbornly resists these treatments, you can turn to commercial cleaners containing dilute solutions of oxalic or other acids. These cleansers are a last step and should be used with caution. Even though the acids in them are diluted, they are still potentially harmful. Use according to the manufacturer's directions and ventilate any room in which they are used. Avoid skin or eye contact, and flush the surface with clean water thoroughly after using an acid-based cleanser (avoid flushing these types of cleaners into a septic system because they kill beneficial microorganisms).

LIME & SCALE

Older plumbing fixtures have most likely been subjected to mineral-rich hard water, because they were often used with well water or before water-softening systems became widespread. Consequently, a reclaimed tub or sink may have blue, gray, or green stains from mineral deposits that have built up over time. You can often remove these with a simple wash of hydrogen peroxide or bleach. However, do not let these sit on the surface for more than a few minutes because they can dull the shine and roughen the surface. An effective solution for many types of mineral build-up is to dilute a tablespoon of dishwasher soap labeled for preventing water spots with about a half-gallon of water. Scrub the stains with the mixture using a nylon scrub brush and a good amount of elbow grease and the stains should eventually disappear. You'll find many cleansers on the market formulated specifically for lime and mineral deposits. Some work better than others, so you may need to experiment a bit. Many of these contain dilute acid formulations, so exercise the same cautions described above and always follow manufacturer's directions for use and safety precautions.

CLEANING RECLAIMED HARDWARE

Bringing metal doorknobs, hinges, and other hardware back to life starts with a thorough cleaning. Although a few pits or dents in hardware may add to its vintage look, a painted-over surface does not. Some techniques, such as a removing paint from antique hardware, are fairly universal regardless of the metal. Some solutions, such as bringing a high shine back to the surface, will depend on the material on which you're working. In the case of operable fixtures such as doorknobs and hinges, a thorough cleaning is not only a matter of aesthetics, it may also help improve the function of the piece.

Because unfinished metal surfaces are susceptible to damage from harsh cleansers, it's always better to look for simple home remedies or physical means of cleaning hardware. In any case, never use a cleaner or finishing product that is not specifically labeled for the metal. And bear in mind that, much like wood flooring and many other reclaimed materials, retaining some of the patina of age may be a key attraction in the appearance of the piece.

SALVAGE WISDOM: REFINISHING ENAMELED CAST-IRON TUBS

In some cases, the perfect antique cast-iron tub for your bathroom remodel will be too stained or chipped to be rescued with a simple cleaning. Not to worry—that tub can be refinished to look as good as new. The process is fairly straightforward but requires specialized skills and equipment, so tub refinishing is not a DIY project. A reputable professional however, can make an antique tub look like new in a day, for a few hundred dollars. Depending on the tub, that can translate to a savings of hundreds of dollars or more over the cost of a new reproduction vintage tub. The process involves a thorough cleaning with strong cleaning agents, filling chips, cracks, and other physical damage with an epoxy filler, priming the entire surface, and refinishing with a several top coats that are sanded between applications. Done right, the tub will be ready for use that night. If cleaned and maintained properly, a refinished tub can last a decade or more.

REMOVING PAINT

The most common issue with older hardware is layers of paint. It only takes one impatient homeowner or painter to paint over door, cabinet, or other hardware, and everyone thereafter repeats the mistake. The first step to getting the paint off and assessing the metal underneath is removing the hardware from the painted surface. Because the surface itself—such as an old, solid panel door—may be in the process of being salvaged, you need to remove the hardware without damaging the underlying surface or the hardware itself. First cut the paint seal around the borders of the hardware, using an X-acto knife, or a similar fine-edged blade. Then remove the fasteners that hold the hardware in place.

To remove layers of paint, turn to a time-tested solution: cook the hardware. Put the hardware in a disposable aluminum pan half-filled with water and a squirt or two of dishwashing soap. Put the pan on the stove over a burner set to the lowest heat possible, and let the hardware sit in its bath for six hours at least—the longer the better (12 hours will usually work to release the finish on most any painted hardware). The paint should soften as a single layer and will often slide right off the hardware. Remove the hardware from its bath and brush any remaining paint out of nooks and crannies with a stiff toothbrush or small nylon brush, using additional soap and hot water with the brush to remove any stubborn paint. Dry the hardware immediately with a soft clean cloth.

If you are trying to remove a finish such as lacquer, or if you don't have success with the water-and-soap bath, you can soak the hardware in a bath of chemical strippers. Rather than use harsh strippers containing methylene chloride, consider a longer soak in one of the many milder newer formulations, such as soy-based strippers.

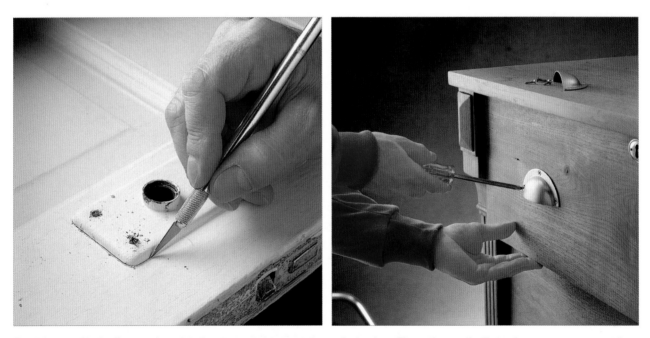

Careful removal is the first step in reclaiming vintage hardware. A thorough cleaning will usually reveal a distinctive accent you can use in many ways.

POLISHING AND REFINISHING HARDWARE

Metals, especially softer metals such as brass or copper, degrade over time when exposed to pollutants in the air, moisture, and even chemicals and dirt on the surface of skin that touches the metal. In some cases, you may find the patina of age on hinges or mounting plates to be attractive. In other instances, you may want your reclaimed hardware to shine like new. The process for refinishing hardware and fixtures varies depending on the type of metal.

BRASS

The first step to cleaning tarnish off brass and polishing the surface is to strip any remaining protective coating. This is done by coating the hardware in a quick bath of lacquer thinner and letting it dry. Then coat the hardware in brass cleaner (several types are available at hardware stores and home centers) according to the manufacturer's directions—this usually involves rubbing on the solution and letting the piece sit for a prescribed amount of time. Clean the brass hardware and then use a bench grinder with a polishing/buffing wheel, and a small amount of brass polish, to shine the brass to your preferred sheen. Always use eye protection when polishing metal on a bench grinder, and use pliers with padded jaws to hold small pieces firmly. Finally, protect the refinished surface with a sprayed-on application of clear lacquer or acrylic urethane (both are available in spray cans from large paint stores or home centers).

COPPER

Strip copper of any protective coating prior to cleaning and polishing. Rub it over the surface with a clean cloth, or use a brush to get at intricate detailing. Remove tarnish with a copper polish or use the proven home method of boiling the hardware in a solution of water with a teaspoon of salt and cup of vinegar. You can also rub a lemon wedge in salt, and then use it to rub over the surface. In any case, after you've removed the tarnish, wash the hardware thoroughly with a mild solution of dish soap and warm water, and dry immediately with a clean, dry cloth. Finish by coating the copper with a protective finish—you'll find several different types at hardware stores and home centers. Follow the manufacturer's directions for application, use and safety precautions.

STEEL & IRON

The most common sign of aging on steel and iron hardware is rust. The quickest way to remove rust and grime from these porous metals is by using a bench grinder with a wire wheel. Use eye protection and gloves. Iron hardware is often painted, providing a finish that is at once decorative and protective. However, you can also spray iron and steel hardware with a protective layer of lacquer or acrylic urethane. As an alternative, a layer of paste wax will protect the surface and is easy to remove should you ever need or want to refinish the surface in the future.

SALVAGING VINTAGE LIGHTING FIXTURES

The first step in updating an older lighting fixture is to disassemble the fixture entirely for cleaning and repair. Clean the exposed metal pieces of the fixture. If the glass portion of the fixture is very dirty, soak in a mild solution of dishwashing soap and warm water. Otherwise, clean the glass with a general glass cleaner.

Inspect the parts of the fixture. If the fixture is more than a few years old, replace the socket and insulator and the ceramic housing and cap. Use new wires connected to the socket, including a ground wire, and use a new crossbar mounting bracket with a grounding screw for ceiling-hung fixtures. With the breaker for the room power switched off, reassemble the fixture. Screw the new wires in place on the new socket, and connect the other ends to the ceiling or wall electrical box. Finally, screw the fixture base onto the crossbar mounting bracket. Turn on the power and test the light.

RESOURCES

Building Materials Reuse Association
A non-profit educational and research organization with the goal of encouraging efficient building deconstruction and the use of reclaimed building materials.
(800) 990-2672
www.bmra.org

Building Green
Organization that offers information, newsletters and other resources on building green, including reuse of reclaimed building materials.
(802) 257-7300
www.buildinggreen.com

The Deconstruction Institute
An organization providing information and tools exploring and explaining deconstruction as an alternative to demolition and adding to the waste stream.
(941) 358-7730
www.deconstructioninstitute.com

The Energy & Environmental Building Alliance (EEBA)
A resource providing information and education about sustainable and environmentally responsible building practices, and an advocate promoting sustainable construction.
(952) 881-1098
www.eeba.org

Forest Stewardship Council (FSC)
Independent non-profit dedicated to responsible management of the world's forests. Provides certification of wood that has been responsibly managed and/or represents environmentally responsible wood products for consumption.
www.fsc.org/about-fsc.html

Habitat for Humanity ReStores
Information about the non-profit's retail outlets selling reclaimed building materials.
www.habitat.org/restores/default.aspx

Reuse Development Organization
A non-profit dedicated to promoting reuse as an environmentally responsible, socially beneficial and economical way to manage solid waste.
(410) 558-3625 ex. 15
loadingdock.org/redo/

U.S Green Building Council
Non-profit organization promoting green building practices and socially responsible waste management—including salvaging, reuse, and reclamation—through information and programs. The council administers LEED (Leadership in Energy and Environmental Design), the standardized, internationally accepted green building rating system.
www.usgbc.org

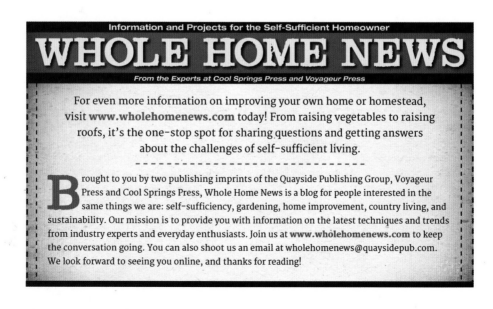

INDEX